D0900073

BACKGROUND FOR QUEEN ANNE

By the Same Author

DEFOE

CHARLOTTE, COUNTESS OF WARWICK

BACKGROUND FOR QUEEN ANNE

by

JAMES SUTHERLAND

With Eight Plates

METHUEN & CO. LTD., LONDON
36 Essex Street, Strand, W.C. 2

First published in 1939

PRINTED IN GREAT BRITAIN

PREFACE

Two hundred years from now, the reader who is interested in the early twentieth century will have no difficulty in finding out all that he wants to know about George V, Earl Haig, Colonel Lawrence, and Mr. Bernard Shaw. History can be trusted to look after her own; and Mr. Shaw—admittedly with excellent material to work upon—has taken good care that he shall not be forgotten. But if the curious reader meets with the name of Horatio Bottomley, or Amy Johnson, or George Robey, or if he comes across a reference to Buchmanism or Aston Villa, he will no doubt experience some difficulty in finding out who or what they were, and why they were so celebrated in their own day. Yet if he wants to understand the early twentieth century, and to know what men and women were really like in that period, he is much more likely to get the right answer by rediscovering the Bottomleys and the Robeys than by fastening his attention exclusively upon their more famous contemporaries.

Of the seven characters about whom I have written in this book, four, I imagine, are quite unknown even to those who are fairly familiar with the eighteenth century. They turned up when I was looking for other things. Richard Burridge, for instance, I first came across when I was reading through *Mist's Weekly Journal*;

and after meeting with him several times in other newspapers of the period, I began to realise that in his own day he was something of a celebrity. Soon afterwards I came across his name again, this time among some documents in the Public Record Office; and when I discovered that he was almost the leading bad man of his generation, and had written a little book all about his dreadful wickedness, my curiosity was thoroughly aroused. If I am asked why I have brought back men like Richard Burridge and John Lacy from the kindly obscurity that had settled over their lives, I must reply that they have attracted me by their persistent vitality. Both of these men were astonishingly alive, and I find little difficulty in thinking of them as still

> imprison'd in the viewlesse windes
> And blowne with restlesse violence round about
> The pendant world.

But apart from their intrinsic worth in terms of personality, they have a value as part of the generation into which they were born. They were worth preserving because they contribute something to the varied background of English life at one of the most remarkable periods in English history. My three other characters are, of course, well known. But in writing of them I am still concerned with the occurrences of every day, and the point of view is still that of the ordinary man. In dealing with Marlborough's funeral, for example, I have described it from the point of view of the man in the street—the point of view, in fact, that I found in the contemporary newspapers. It was not my intention to belittle the great or to be facetious about the obscure, but there is nothing more likely to give one a sense of detachment than a prolonged reading of daily or weekly journals more than two hundred years old. The short items of news that appear between each of my separate studies were compiled from the various newspapers of Queen Anne's reign ; they should help the reader to build up in his own mind that social and political background that I have tried to re-create.

With fiction I have had no dealings ; not consciously, at any rate. Having set out to write biography, I have made it as interesting as I can without troubling to imagine events and conversations which in fact never took place at all. I confess to a crude and probably inartistic concern for things that have actually happened ; and this interest is partly due, though not exclusively so, to the fact that they *have* happened. Again, I have not tried to make my dead men more exciting or picturesque than they actually were. It is apparently a natural human desire that the dead should live again ; it is a weakness of modern biography to make them more lively than they ever were in life. If this sounds unnecessarily pedantic, I can only answer that biography to-day is badly in need of a little whalebone to discipline a too ample figure. I have written about my seven characters because they interested or amused me. The fact that they are dead, and cannot answer me back, has not made me tender of their reputation ; I hope it has made me careful of my facts, and cautious in my interpretation of them.

The portrait of Charlotte, Countess of Warwick, is reproduced by kind permission of the owner, Mrs. G. J. Jackson, of Great Posbrooke, Titchfield, Hants. To her, and to Major Hedworth T. Barclay and Major G. J. Jackson for their courteous assistance in this connection, I should like to offer my sincere thanks. I am also indebted to Mr. H. M. Cashmore, F.L.A., City Librarian, Birmingham Public Libraries, for directing my attention to the illustration of Bilton Hall.

LONG WITTENHAM,

January, 1939

CONTENTS

ILLUSTRATIONS

Oh it is a goodly thing to learne the Theorike of such as understand the practice well. But forsomuch as the Sermon is one thing and the Preacher an other, I love as much to see Brutus in Plutarke as in himself: I would rather make choice to know certainly what talk he had in his tent with some of his familiar friends, the night fore-going the battell, than the speech he made the morrow after to his Armie; and what he did in his chamber or closet, than what in the senate or market place.

Montaigne, *Of Bookes* (Florio's translation, 1603)

CURRENT INTELLIGENCE

1700–1702

Her Royal Highness, the Princess of Denmark, who had the misfortune to Miscarry of a Prince on Wednesday Morning, is as well as her condition will permit.

On Monday last, Mrs. Lane, an ancient woman in Duck-Lane, had her throat cut by some that lodg'd in her House.

The Skeleton and Bones of the great Whale, lately taken in the River Thames, being now well dried, clean'd, and exactly put together, may be seen daily in a large Booth in West Smithfield. The price is put at 3d.

The Pope has kept his bed ever since the 13th.

On Tuesday last His Majesty took the Divertisement of Hunting etc. about Hampton Court.

The dead Warrant has come down to Newgate for the Execution of four Men and two Women tomorrow at Tyburn.

There is now made publick for the general Good, That famous Medicine, called Aqua-anti-Torminalis, being an incomparable Water against all manner of Gripings of the Guts, Wind, Chollick, or Dry-Belly-Ach.

Yesterday Morning between 4 and 5, His Majesty Signified to his Grace the Archbishop of Canterbury that he was sensible his Death was approaching . . . and about 8 a clock that Morning our Gracious Sovereign Lord, King William III, Our Glorious Deliverer from Popery and Slavery, Surrendered his Soul to God at his Pallace at Kensington. . . .

Christened this Week, 284, buried, 399.

Lost the 29th instant from St. James's Place, a little white Bitch, long tailed, very fat, with brown Ears, and large brown spots on each side. . . .

Thence they proceeded to Temple Bar, where, being met by the Lord Mayor, Aldermen, and Sherriffs of London, Her Majesty was Proclaim'd a third time. All the Streets, Windows, and Balconies were crowded with vast numbers of Spectators.

Sir Cloudsley Shovel is in the Downs with 13 *men of war.*

This Morning a young Bigbelly'd Woman hang'd her self upon the staple of one of the posts of Bear Binder Lane.

Yesterday an Order was Published, by Her Majestie's Royal Pleasure, That all Persons, upon the Death of his late Majesty King William, do put them selves in the deepest Mourning that may be. . . . And that for the Incouragement of our English Lutestring and A-la-mode Manufacture, Hatbands of black English A-la-mode, cover'd with Crape, will be allow'd as full and proper Mourning.

On Monday last nine Malefactors were executed at Chelmsford in Essex.

The best Wheat 4*s. per Bushel, Rye* 3*s.* 3*d. Barley per Quarter* 20*s. Oats* 14*s. Coals* 23*s. per Chaldron.*

Pulvus Mirabilis. . . . One Dose of its Powder, with the Blessing of God, cures the most inveterate P—x in a Fortnight's time or less.

Whereas Judith Ustick, aged 33 *Years, a short, thick Woman, a little Crooked and Waddles much in Going, brown Hair, long Face, a full under Lipp . . .*

Yesterday eight Malefactors were executed at Tyburn. . . .

Burridge the Blasphemer

A pox o' your throat, you bawling, blasphemous, incharitable dog!
The Tempest

TOWARDS the close of the seventeenth century there was living in London a certain Mary Burridge who must sometimes have looked with surprise and a certain dismay at what she had done. The boy, her little boy, who had once tottered about the floor and climbed upon chairs and tables so precariously, who was once so weak and helpless and easily hurt, had grown up to manhood, and had turned out, quite unaccountably but not the less certainly, a wrong one. Indeed, his wickedness was such as to make him a byword among his contemporaries. The really black sheep is as rare a phenomenon among men as it is among sheep, and for that reason something of a curiosity. Too many promising scoundrels are spoilt through some irrelevant streak of generosity or affection, some amiable weakness of character which keeps them from the worst excesses. But every now and then a child is born who proceeds with unwavering steps to a career of complete, and therefore oddly satisfactory, wickedness. Of those rare creatures, one of the most complete in his own small way was Richard Burridge, better known in his own day as Burridge the Blasphemer, a man so repulsive in almost every respect as to become very nearly attractive.

The contemporaries of Richard Burridge may well have believed that his name would descend to the latest generations as an awful warning; but neither the student of literature nor the historian has seen any good reason for remembering him, and he has faded with all his works from human memory. Had Pope only given him, as well he might, a line or two in *The Dunciad*, Burridge would have lingered on, a fly in the poet's amber; but he escaped *The Dunciad*, and so lost his surest chance of fame. When he was forty-two he had a fit of repentance, and sat down to write a conscientious account of his own evil life, which he called *Religio Libertini: or The Faith of a Converted Atheist*. Burridge, however, was no Bunyan, and his little book is hardly more than a curiosity. That, perhaps, is about all that can be said for Burridge himself; and yet he is so odd a creature, so nearly fictitious—something created by Smollett almost, or at any rate by Smollett collaborating with Samuel Richardson—that he deserves to have his memory preserved.

On May 16, 1670, about two o'clock in the afternoon, the wife of Edward Burridge, a respectable citizen of the parish of St. Martin's in the Fields, was delivered of her son. It is possible to be so precise because Richard Burridge has given us his own word for it; no doubt he copied the facts from the family Bible. His childhood was all that the most exacting parents could wish. Quite early he began to distinguish himself by a constant application to his studies. He was a weak and sickly child; and so, while other and more robust children were merely growing bigger and stronger, he was making steady progress with his books. Such is the advantage of a delicate constitution, that by the time he was sixteen he knew all about Mathematics and Astronomy, and was perfectly familiar with the Latin and Greek poets. Or so he says, and it makes little difference whether he is telling the truth or not: the significance of Burridge lies elsewhere. So far all was going well, indeed very well. His parents had brought him up piously in sound Church of England principles. His father, intending him for the Church, got so far as to take him to Oxford, where he hoped to enter him as a gentleman commoner of Magdalen; but Magdalen was at that time in a state of confusion owing to the efforts of James II to force a Catholic Master upon the fellows, and the visit came to nothing. Oxford had to do without young Burridge.

It was just about this time, if we are to believe his own account, that he started to go wrong. He began to frequent a Catholic seminary in the Savoy, and there he had ample opportunities of showing off those intellectual attainments of which he was already so conscious. He engaged in frequent arguments with his new Jesuit friends, and invariably confuted what he calls "their erroneous tenets." But he was playing with fire. In spite of all his intellectual victories, he was at last won over by their persistence, and consented to become a Catholic. What his parents thought about the visits of their clever son to the Catholic seminary he does not say; but he managed to conceal from them his change of faith. His prospects of advancement were now decidedly hopeful. A Catholic King must have some employment for a promising young Catholic scholar, and James had already had the pleasure of listening to a Latin speech read before him by young Burridge when he made an official visit to the Seminary. But when Burridge was still only eighteen, James spoilt everything by suddenly taking flight from his kingdom, and the young Catholic found himself cold-shouldered by a rabble of triumphant Protestants.

And now began the real descent to the moral abyss. Young Burridge took to the pleasures of the Town, he frequented the tavern, the playhouse, balls and masquerades. We hear no more of his delicate constitution. As the soul grew sick, the body became more and more robust; he had obviously outgrown the queasiness of his childhood. He learnt now to fence, and in a short time became so expert in what he calls "the bloody art of defacing God's image," that he would quarrel with any man upon the least provocation. In all, he fought eighteen duels—or, once again, so he says—and never received a single wound. At night, like Etheredge's Sir Frederick Frollick, he would wander about the fashionable quarter of the Town with his dissolute companions, serenading the whores, bilking coachmen, breaking windows, beating the watch. His parents were indulgent and apparently unsuspecting; they gave him all the money he asked for, and he spent it on women. Among his companions he had a reputation for his bawdy verses; they called him "young Rochester," and encouraged him in his evil courses. He was young, he was clever, he had plenty of money to spend, and he was not afraid to flourish his sword. For the present, the world—or, at any rate, his own little world of whores and taverns, the theatre and the coffee-house—was at his feet. Old Mr. Burridge had long since ceased to exercise any effective control over his son, and early in 1691, while young Burridge was in the full course of his debauchery, the old man died. The "young Rochester" was stunned into writing a short elegy; and one must hope that his bawdy verses reached a higher standard than those which he now wrote to commemorate a parent. "Methinks," he concludes,

> Methinks I hear descending Angels cry,
> Ascend, blest BURRIDGE, to thy native Sky;
> For 'till you mount yon bright seraphick Seat,
> The Joys of Heaven cannot be compleat.

Mr. Burridge's death had clearly been a shock to his son, who was still only twenty-one ; but the check was only momentary. He soon returned with renewed zest to the old dissolute life, to the playhouse and the tavern, the duelling and the wenching. One day, however, he got a sharp fright. When "taking water" at Westminster Bridge, he handed his mistress into the boat and leapt in after her. Unfortunately the young woman was still standing up at her end of the boat as Burridge jumped in at the other ; and when the boat lurched suddenly under the weight of her lover she not unnaturally lost her balance and fell in the river. Burridge, still in the boat, attempted to pull her out, but the terrified woman clutched so desperately at the lapel of his coat that she ended by dragging him into the water too. Though he was unable to swim he managed to keep struggling on the surface, and at last some watermen succeeded in drawing them both ashore. He had been warned ; but this signal example of God's mercy had no effect on a hardened sinner.

Mrs. Burridge was now much concerned about her son's future, and about this time she succeeded in entering him at the Inner Temple and procuring him chambers in Symond's Inn. Burridge, however, wasted very little time in reading law ; and when his laundress found him in bed one morning with a wench, and informed the proper authorities, he decided to give up the study of law altogether. For another year the rake's progress continued. "Nothing," he writes, "could put me in mind of mortality but the ringing of bells, which still make me naturally melancholly." But for the present he succeeded in stopping his ears pretty effectively. He had now transferred his attention from whores to the wives and daughters of respectable citizens, a natural enough progress for the experienced roué, and one which his familiarity with the contemporary drama must have made easy. He seems, however, to have managed his amours less adroitly than the imperturbable young rakes of Etheredge and Congreve ; for on one occasion a friend of his refused to play the game properly, and brought a suit against him for eloping with his wife—a sordid eventuality which never darkens the glittering activity of a Restoration comedy. But it happened to Burridge, and it proved a troublesome business ; he was arrested, and spent eleven weeks in confinement.

In 1692, however, when he was still only twenty-two, he took a wife of his own. Yet it was not, apparently, with any intention of settling down ; for soon afterwards he joined an expedition which was setting out under the command of Sir Francis Wheler to capture the French island of Martinique in the West Indies. The account of his life which Burridge wrote in 1712 is so typically that of the reformed sinner that it is scarcely surprising to learn that almost as soon as the expedition started he had another solemn warning from heaven : his ship ran into a dreadful storm in the Bay of Biscay. The Bay of Biscay, indeed, seems to have had few calm moments in the seventeenth and eighteenth centuries. One is almost tempted to believe that it was placed there to bring sinners to repentance ; it certainly opened the way to much characteristic moralising. Not, however, on this occasion : Burridge deliberately rejected the opportunity for self-examination which this particular storm offered. "In the most dreadful and terrible tempest," he writes, "I audaciously outbrav'd the thoughts of it, by playing at cards, dice, draughts, tables, or mungus." One is not therefore altogether unprepared for the next appalling development : he became an atheist. He even went so far as to give up his soul in a fit of bravado to the Devil, formally signing the document with his own blood. Though there was no God, there was still apparently a Devil to be believed in ; but there is perhaps no contradiction here, for Burridge's atheism seems to have been of the sort that prompts a man to be rude to his God rather than to disbelieve in His existence. It is well to profit by the mistakes of other men, and Burridge tells us how this change was wrought in him : he became an atheist after reading Lucretius and Lucian's dialogues,

> which pernicious authors so poison'd my reason, that publickly denying the being of a Deity and the tenets of a resurrection, judgment, Heaven or Hell, I have made my auditors stand amaz'd.

The clue to a good deal of Burridge's behaviour lies in his obvious delight in amazing his auditors. He was a boastful creature, and he liked to parade his wits and his erudition.

The expedition to the West Indies was not a success ; indeed, Sir Francis Wheler and his subordinates made a sorry hash of things. Wheler was a brave man and a competent sailor, but he was dogged with ill-luck, and hampered by a divided command. Nominally, he was in command of the entire expedition, but the army took its orders from Colonel Foulkes, and the two men were not always in agreement about what place they should attack and how they should go about it. Before he had set sail Wheler had asked that ample provision should be made for treating the sick, for he knew how dangerous the climate of the West Indies could be to Englishmen, and he had heard that the plague was raging at Barbados. On his arrival at Barbados, however, with twelve men-of-war and two regiments of soldiers, he was assured by the Governor that the island had never been healthier, and accordingly the men were taken ashore and billeted in private houses. A few of the seamen sickened, but most of the soldiers were in excellent health. Some weeks later the fleet set sail for Martinique, and there the English force was joined by Colonel Codrington at the head of two Creole regiments from the Leeward Islands.

For several days the English troops were employed in nothing more difficult than destroying the sugar plantations along the coast and setting fire to outlying buildings; but on Sunday, April 17, the whole army was disembarked in perfect order near St. Pierre, and camped at some distance from the town. On Monday morning the first real fighting took place. Marching out from St. Pierre, the French drove back several of the English advance parties that had wandered too far ahead, and soon the whole of Colonel Foulkes' little army was engaged with the enemy. For three or four hours there was a warm musketry fire on both sides, and then the fighting died down. At the end of the day Wheler reckoned his losses at 130 killed and wounded. Burridge, who took part in the fighting, describes the engagement as "a bloody battle," and puts the English losses at 500 killed. The French, one hardly needs to be told, were infinitely superior in numbers, and lost three times as many men. There was so little of either glory or profit in Wheler's abortive expedition to the West Indies that it is comforting to learn that in this engagement before St. Pierre one Englishman behaved with outstanding bravery. This was Richard Burridge: we have his own word for it. "In this sharp dispute," he tells us, "it was observ'd by Admiral Wheler I behav'd with such an undaunted bravery and courage, although the dead fell like hops on the right and left of me, that he was pleas'd to make me his Secretary."

When the light came in on Tuesday morning, it was seen that the French had withdrawn behind their fortifications. Wheler landed two of his cannon and proceeded to bombard the town ; the French replied by firing cannon balls into the English camp. The following day Colonel Foulkes went reconnoitring for some distance inland, and one of his companies meeting with a body of French settlers quite shamefully ran away. "Colonel Foulkes, with his sword in his hand," Wheler wrote to the Lords of the Admiralty, "had much ado to stop a rout." Something had gone wrong with the English troops ; perhaps they were already beginning to sicken for the plague. English cannon balls, however, continued to bounce into St. Pierre, and French cannon balls came thudding at intervals into the English camp. On Thursday morning Admiral Wheler called a council of war. Colonel Foulkes was all for leaving St. Pierre alone and attacking at some other point ; Wheler was for staying where they were and battering the French and their town to pieces with the big guns from his ships. There was a warm debate, but only two officers supported Wheler, and at last he was forced to give way. By three A.M. on Saturday morning the troops had all been re-embarked, and the ships were under sail. The expedition to the West Indies had shot its bolt ; Wheler never got a chance to strike another blow.

On Sunday the fleet anchored off Dominica. Two days later Wheler called his officers together for another council of war, and again he was heavily outvoted. He wanted now to attack Gaudeloupe, but he got no support for this project either, and he was forced to set sail for

St. Christopher in the Leeward Islands. On its way there the fleet came to the island of Montserrat, and here an incident occurred which Burridge recorded with real satisfaction ; it was evidently one of the big moments of his life. "Reaching Montserrat," he tells us, "the whole Fleet lay by, till Sir Francis Wheler and I went to take a repast ashore for three or four Hours."

The retreat to St. Christopher—for it was a retreat—was perhaps the best move that Admiral Wheler could make under the circumstances. The plague that he had been dreading before he left England had broken out among his ships, and his men were sickening at an alarming rate. The sight of his messmates dying daily of a sudden and terribly rapid disease was enough to sober down the most abandoned reprobate ; but Burridge merely laughed and went on with his drinking. "So hardened was I amidst my cups," he writes, "that I made it but a mere scoff and a May-game, to see poor men lie bleeding to death at the fundament above deck, and thrown nine or ten in a day overboard for a bait to the fish, which lay in the deep receptacles of the vast ocean." By the middle of May Wheler had lost half his sailors. "We have made but a bad hand," he wrote frankly to a friend in England, "and it will doubtless make a noise in the world." In the fleet alone the plague had carried off seven commanders, three lieutenants, three masters, seven gunners, eleven captains, eight pursers, seven bosuns, eight surgeons, eleven carpenters, nine cooks, and more than six hundred seamen. As for the army, the colonels of both regiments were dead, together with a major, seven captains, and about twenty subalterns, and of the rank and file, there were only about six hundred and fifty left alive.

But Burridge lived on : perhaps his hearty drinking

preserved him from infection. At last the epidemic burnt itself out, and with his shattered and dispirited squadron Wheler set sail for New England, hoping to obtain a sufficient number of recruits for an attack on Quebec. He arrived at Boston about the middle of June, but his plans for an attack in Canada aroused no enthusiasm in the Governor, who told him that he had no men to spare for such an expedition. Wheler, who was rapidly turning into a sort of English Ulysses, now set his course for Newfoundland, intending to attack Placentia. But here again his luck was out; the town was too strongly fortified to be attacked by the discouraged convalescents that he had at his disposal, and there was nothing for it but to return to England. Towards the middle of October, with hardly enough men left to navigate the ships, Wheler sighted the coast of Ireland. He had done his best, and accomplished almost nothing. But he must have had good friends at the Admiralty, for instead of being disgraced he was almost immediately put in command of another fleet for service in the Mediterranean. On December 27 he set sail, but his ill-luck still pursued him. On February 19 he ran into a hurricane off Malaga, and his flagship, the "Sussex," went down at five o'clock in the morning with 550 men on board. That was the end of Admiral Wheler, and it would undoubtedly have been the end of Burridge too if he had remained in Wheler's service; but fortunately for himself he had resigned his post as soon as he returned to England.

Burridge was lucky; but though he had escaped a hero's death by drowning he very nearly met a less spectacular end in his bed. Back in England, he and his wife both caught the spotted fever, and only recovered after a dangerous illness. For the next two years he appears to have lived quietly in the country, and then the idea occurred to him that his mother might want to see him again. He found the old lady in mourning weeds, for she had been told that he had been lost at sea, and as he had never written to her nor made any attempt to communicate with her she not unnaturally believed him to be dead. Burridge is at some pains to paint the joyful reunion and the tears that were shed on both sides. What he shed tears for he does not say; but he will have it that he was overjoyed to see his mother, and he must be allowed to be the best judge of his feelings. Three years later she followed her husband to the grave, and again Burridge paused in his career to mourn in verse for a lost parent.

About this time he had another of his providential escapes. One dark night when he was riding over a bridge that had no parapet, he and his horse tumbled together into the river below. The stream was running high, swollen with recent rains, and he was almost swept away; but the horse managed to bring him to the bank, and he scrambled to safety. Once again he had been warned, and again he disregarded the voice of Heaven.

In the year of the Jubilee he set out by himself for Rome, leaving his wife to look after the children. He reached Holland safely, but at The Hague he fell in with some gentlemen and proceeded to gamble with them until he had lost all his money. The journey to Rome was now impossible, and without some money in his pocket it was equally impossible for him to return to England. At this crisis, however, a Dutch lady at the Brill, Madam Huggerswart, took compassion on him, and after entertaining him for some time in her house gave him sufficient money to return home. How

Burridge repaid this kindness he does not say; perhaps he considers it self-evident. But as he makes no boast of a conquest, it is possible that the friendship was entirely platonic, and that Madam Huggerswart was kind to the stranger without being false to her husband.

About 1700 he seems to have turned to writing for his livelihood. He published several poems, including a satire on lawyers and physicians which he called *Hell in an Uproar*. Burridge is no poet, but here and there he shows a crude imagination that is rather uncommon in 1700. His picture of Hell is vivid enough:

> I saw to my Amaze the Ghastful Fates;
> On Convex Mounts of Ice, deep Sulphrous Lakes,
> Where Furies with their Hairs of Hissing Snakes
> Tortur'd condemnèd Ghosts with Rods of Fire;
> Plung'd 'em in Surges of Eternal Ire:
> Others in concave Rocks were chain'd, which Waves
> Of boiling Brimstone dasht against. . . .

And he describes the bottom of the sea with a vividness which may owe something to Admiral Wheler's ill-fated expedition to the West Indies:

> There Syrens on soft Beds of Sand were laid,
> And Tritons under Coral-Arbours play'd.
> Most monstrous Fish went rolling through the Waves;
> And Ships lay rotting in those deepless Graves.

But there is little in his career up to this time to prepare one for the book he now published. On July 24, 1700, the little Duke of Gloucester, the last surviving child of the Princess Anne (soon to be better known as Queen Anne), reached his eleventh birthday amidst popular rejoicing. Five days later he was dead. All the poets were at once busy writing odes and elegies, and among the rest, Burridge, the "young Rochester" of a few years ago, addressed the bereaved Princess in a prose pamphlet which he called *The Consolation of Death*.[1] Having made up his mind to do the thing, Burridge proceeded to do it thoroughly. His dedication to the Princess, whatever feelings it may have aroused in the grief-stricken mother, must certainly have given satisfaction to the author; it moves with the courtly circumstance of one who begins by bowing out of respect, and ends by continuing to perform the motions as a delightful means of self-expression. The profounder the obeisance, the more Burridge is enjoying himself. The Epistle Dedicatory is like a blast of muted trumpets:

> The immature dissolution of the late hopeful Branch has caused weeping grief to fly over this Island, for which unexpressible loss can not we be happy till Death transports us to the Celestial Regions, where we may eternally be admiring that object, which the whole Nation so much adored whilst surviving: the absence of such a sacred Child (without whose conversation the joyes of Angels could not be compleat) must needs cut to the heart.

It would be hopeless, Burridge admits, to suggest any comfort to such distress:

> I only attempt to lay this tractate of the Consolation of Death on the shrine of your benign favour, because it was occasionally written on the late unhappy misfortune of ENGLAND, for I am highly sensible that any thing of devotion finds grace in your sight, whose dazling beams of unparallel'd godliness strike your admiring beholders with as much stupefaction, as the brightness of the overshadowing cloud did the amazed disciples on Mount Tabor.

The consolation that Burridge has to offer follows the traditional lines. The Princess is mourning for the death of her son—but then, is life so very fine a thing after

[1] If, indeed, this pamphlet *is* by our Burridge, and not by some other person of the same name.

all? And death, is it so terrible—death that "delivers Infants from running into actual sin, Youth from filling the catalogue of abominable vices, Mankind from the incumbrances of worldly affairs, and Old Age from supporting his tottering frailty on the crutch?" Warming to his task, Burridge goes on to quote freely from the Scriptures, and to cite examples from Plutarch, Seneca, and other authorities, until, in his anxiety to emphasise the wretchedness of this life, he almost presents the Princess with a complete argument for suicide. The little Prince has died in his infancy, but what of it?

> How many feeling extremities a man goes through before his life reaches the winter of hoary age, which makes a strange transformation of his weak nature, his head shaking, his sight dimm, his jaws fallen, his gums toothless, his veins wither'd, his marrow dry'd, his bones sapless, his stomach phlegmatick, his joynts feeble, his limbs numb'd, his blood cold, in a word the whole machine of his feeble body out of order, so it may be said without offence to Heaven, it is better for that man that must be born, to meet his grave as soon as he enters the verge of this troublesome, and always perplexed life.

What the Princess thought of it all one will never know, but Burridge afterwards spoke proudly of favours he had received from her both as Princess and as Queen.

He had still, however, some hopes of a more active career than that of authorship. Early in the reign of Queen Anne he was running four press gangs in an endeavour to round up enough recruits to man a third-rate ship-of-war. In six days he had got together almost two hundred men, but the expense of maintaining the press gangs drained away so much of his money that he had nothing left for purchasing his commission. This was apparently his last attempt to live by his sword; but he never forgot his brief connection with the Navy,

2

for when in 1714 he wrote a little book outlining a method of discovering the longitude, he described himself on the title-page as "R.B., Secretary to the Hon. Sir Francis Wheler." But from about his thirtieth year Burridge was to busy himself with literature—or, not to put it too high, with writing. And even in this comparatively peaceful pursuit he was constantly finding himself in trouble. In 1702 he was so indiscreet as to parody the Church catechism in a libel which he wrote on the Dutch, and for this he was fined, sentenced to stand in the pillory, and imprisoned for twelve months. A week before his release his sister Sarah died of a broken heart. Once again the poetic madness laid hold of him, and he composed another of his family elegies, concluding with the pious wish,

> But when the dreadful Trump shall sound,
> T'awake the sleeping Nations round,
> Then do I hope our Meeting Place
> Will be before the Throne of Grace.

Not long afterwards he was in trouble again, this time for writing an indecent pamphlet. On this occasion he was invited by the Lord Mayor, Sir William Withers, to get out of London and stay out of it. Realising that it would be wise to withdraw for the present, he went over to Ireland. A little later he crossed to Scotland, where he was entertained most civilly by the Universities of Glasgow and Edinburgh. Burridge's life is full of such contradictions as this, and it is clear that he was morally and intellectually a sort of Janus, looking alternately towards good and evil. At one time he is the pious mourner, the competent secretary, the learned and amiable guest who delighted the professors at Edinburgh; the next, he is the drunken rake, the ribald and indecent scribbler whose writings would have shocked the professors if they had known of their existence. Fortunately, Edinburgh was separated from London by a journey of several days, and Burridge's reputation had not yet crossed the Border. He was a stranger, and he had taken them in; or perhaps it was the other Burridge who visited Scotland, while the ghost of the rake and atheist was left to flit emptily about his old haunts in London. As he was leaving the country, he had another of his providential escapes from drowning; he was going aboard ship at Leith when he fell over the quay at high water. Once again, however, he was pulled to safety. Those only too frequent stumblings into the water may, of course, have had a purely accidental origin; but it is hard to avoid a suspicion that on this occasion, at any rate, he had taken leave of Edinburgh when the professors were in an unusually hospitable mood.

In April, 1709, he returned to London and to fresh troubles; and in 1711 he found himself in the Gatehouse, a prisoner for debt. If the Gatehouse was no worse than the average London prison of the early eighteenth century, it was bad enough. When in 1729 the House of Commons inquired into the state of the prisons in London, the most appalling conditions were revealed. At the Marshalsea, for instance, the prisoners were being daily subjected to the most inhuman treatment. In the Common Side it was found that thirty or forty prisoners were being kept in a single room not sixteen feet square and only eight feet high. As the area was not sufficient to allow all those people to lie on the floor at the same time, half of them slept on hammocks slung from the walls, while the rest lay on the wooden boards beneath them. "The air," it was reported, "is so wasted by the number of persons who breathe in that narrow compass, that it is not sufficient to keep them from stifling, several having in the heat of summer perished for want of air." The prisoners were locked up at eight o'clock in the winter and nine o'clock in the summer, and the door was not opened again until morning. In this room of sixteen feet square there was, of course, no kind of lavatory, and the conditions often became indescribable. Gaol distemper carried off hundreds of prisoners every year, and many others actually died of starvation. Torture was not unknown, and every form of brutality was practised by the warders if they happened to take some dislike to a prisoner.

What went on in the Marshalsea went on in varying degrees in the other prisons. When Burridge entered the Gatehouse it was in charge of a certain William Taylor, who seems to have been a typically unpleasant character. Like most of his fellow-wardens, he made the most shocking profits out of his prisoners; those who could afford to pay for such luxuries as beer were scandalously overcharged, and those who had no money at all were in danger of starving to death. Taylor was in the habit, too, of locking up prisoners for debt in a room without any window, and keeping them there for days on end, and he mismanaged his prison disgracefully on several occasions. In May, 1711, not many months before Burridge arrived, a woman prisoner had died in the Gatehouse, and Taylor had allowed her body to remain for over two weeks unburied in a cell until it caused the other prisoners the utmost distress.

The last man to put up quietly with this sort of treatment was Richard Burridge. Whatever else he was, he was no coward, and he had a strong sense of his own importance, and of what was due to him. It is hardly surprising, therefore, that almost at once he fell foul of

William Taylor. The man did not know his place, and Burridge undertook to teach him it. He could not have done anything more indiscreet. The Keeper of a Prison is not to be bullied, and he has unusual opportunities of getting his own back for any insult that may be offered him. Taylor was now waiting for his chance, and it was not long in coming. In his sober hours Burridge's conversation was decent enough, and had even impressed the professors of Edinburgh and Glasgow; but in his cups he was apt to use the most appalling language. Ever since entering the Gatehouse he had been drinking heavily with one or two disreputable companions, and one night several of his fellow-prisoners heard him blaspheming in his liquor in a particularly noisy and shocking fashion. Unfortunately for Burridge, blasphemy was a serious offence, punishable by severe penalties if the accused was convicted; and William Taylor saw in his prisoner's unruly language an excellent means of obtaining his revenge. He had no difficulty in persuading four witnesses to swear in a court of law that they had heard the prisoner using the most blasphemous expressions. He was accused, in fact, of drinking in the company of several other persons "a health to the confusion of Almighty God, a health to the Devil our master, and damnation to the Resurrection." If Burridge ever uttered those words—and it is quite probable that he did—they were undoubtedly due, as one humane witness suggested, to excessive drinking of gin, "which he and his company had in by whole quarts at a time." At best, however, that was an explanation, not an excuse, and Burridge had to take his chance in the court of law.

At his trial he defended himself ably and resolutely, insisting that the charge had been trumped up by the

Keeper of the Prison because of a grudge he bore him, and pointing out to the Court that of the four witnesses called against him, one was a man "who would talk more debauchery in a day than even Rochester writ in a year," another had been committed to the Gatehouse for saying that the Queen was the Duke of Marlborough's gallant, a third was in prison for wounding the Marquess of Carmaerthen, and the fourth was a notorious sodomist. It was perhaps the best line of defence to take, but it did not bring him off. The Court decided to overlook the miscellaneous imperfection of the four witnesses, and found the charge proven. He was sentenced to stand three days in the pillory, and to suffer a year's imprisonment. Blasphemy, indeed, was a dangerous form of indulgence in 1712; the Societies for the Reformation of Manners had been very active in suppressing it, and their efforts had the full approval of the Queen herself. Did she recollect, as her guilty subject served his sentence in the pillory at Charing Cross, the manly little volume that he had written a few years before to console her in her sad bereavement?

Upon Burridge himself the sentence seemed at first to be having a remarkable effect; the pillory was justifying itself, the long months in prison were awaking him to a true repentance. Some of his leisure time, at any rate, he employed in writing that most interesting work, *Religio Libertini*, in which he reviewed the enormities of his past life, and encouraged himself to strive after better things in the future. The world, he reflected, was now hastening to its appointed end; men would not be writing and talking so much to-day if they did not realise that they could not hope to write and talk much longer.

What should we do, then, since we know the world truly old, and now going upon its great, and final climacterick ; but as discreet men would carry themselves to impotent and decrepit age, I'll bear with the infirmities of it, pity and bewail the distemper, strive against the enormities, and prepare for the dissolution.

To one shut up in a London prison in the year 1712, and watching the dull winter afternoons fade out on the bare boards of the floor, the world might well seem to be running down to that final and inevitable hour. There is much in *Religio Libertini* that points to the genuine repentance of a converted sinner. Burridge sees the hand of God in his present unhappy circumstances ; God has arranged everything so that His unworthy servant may be brought to his senses. There are ample protestations of abhorrence for his past wickedness, large promises for the future. But to the practical evangelist, if *Religio Libertini* fell into the hands of any such, there must have been some grounds for misgiving. In his very insistence on the awful sins he had committed, Burridge betrays a pride not yet fully chastened. He is " the greatest atheist in the last or present age," he tells us, and one feels that it is the greatness rather than the atheism that he is thinking of as he writes. It is the same when he is dealing with his affairs of gallantry ; he narrates them with an unmistakable relish, and one feels again that the emphasis is on the past joys rather than on the present repentance. Can it be that Burridge was only writing a catchpenny pamphlet, designed to allure the light-minded with a lively picture of vice? To believe so is to miss the most interesting side of his character ; he *is* the repentant sinner, but his new-found humility is shot through with pagan streaks of vanity still. The joys of the reformed profligate are not entirely those of self-abasement ; there is something, too, of an inward satisfaction that one could have been so bad. And though Burridge humbles himself before his God, he is still concerned to make an impressive appearance before the eyes of his fellow-men.

At all events his little book is full of earnest resolutions to make up by a blameless life in the years to come for the wickedness of his youth. At the age of forty-two he renounces all the vain joys of this world, and publicly encourages himself to set his affections on things above. His soul is sick ; it can be healed only by the great Physician.

> Alas ! the *Dog*, when he is stomach-sick, can go right to his proper *grass ;* the *Cat* to her *nep ;* the *Goat* to his *hemlock ;* the *Weasel* to *rice ;* the *Hart* to *dittany ;* but now I am mortally soul-sick, and naturally know no remedy for my distemper ; oh ! thou that art the great *Physician* in Heaven, first cure my insensibleness ; make thou me as sick of my sins, as I have made my self sick by sin, and then speak the word, and I shall be whole again.

Had he persevered with this mood there would probably be nothing further to record of Burridge ; but forty-two is no great age, and when the prison doors opened at last, and he walked out once more upon the sunny streets, he seems to have recovered his spirits. Had he been sixty-two, things might have been different ; but at two-and-forty the blood still runs strong, and there are hasty words to be made good, and blows to be returned.

For the next few years, however, he managed to keep out of trouble. He found a job on a Whig paper, *Read's Weekly Journal ;* and though Read, in view of what afterwards happened, was always eager to make out that Burridge was only a corrector for the press, he certainly wrote for this paper. He was living now with his wife and family in a court off Drury Lane, a notorious district full of the sort of attractions that Burridge was least fitted to resist. Up to the year 1718 he seems to have lived quietly and peaceably; but early in that year the Devil again tempted him, and once again he fell. About two o'clock one February morning he came reeling back to his lodging, appallingly drunk. There was no crime in that, but unfortunately Burridge woke up all the neighbours with his knocking, and they could hear him cursing and swearing in the street. His wife tried to quieten him, and did, in fact, manage to get him upstairs to his room; but he then proceeded to beat her, and made towards the door as if he meant to go out again. This was just what his wife wanted above all to prevent, and she asked him anxiously where he was going. Burridge's reply must undoubtedly have relieved his feelings: "To Hell!" he told her. "Good God!" exclaimed poor Mrs. Burridge. "What will become of you?" It was then that Burridge uttered his grand blasphemy, and reached in one sudden burst of insolence the culminating point of his career. "I can go to Hell when I please," he told his wife with maudlin dignity, "and come out again at my pleasure. D—mn G—d A—y, if I had Him here, I would stick Him to the heart." This was going too far, even in Drury Lane, and Burridge was removed to prison.

At his trial he called his son as a witness for him; and the boy, while admitting that his father came home very drunk, denied that he swore a single oath, or, in fact, said anything at all, except "that he would smoak his pipe; and that he sat down, and immediately fell asleep, and the pipe dropt out of his mouth." But in spite of this highly circumstantial evidence, and the testimony of several other witnesses who assured the Court that Burridge was "a modest peaceable man when sober, never using any vile expressions, but when drunk was a perfect madman, and that the least matter of drink immaginable wou'd put him into that disorder," the Court was not prepared to overlook the present offence. On March 7, 1718, he was convicted of blasphemy for the second time, and sentenced to be whipped by the common hangman from the New Church in the Strand to Charing Cross. It was generally felt that his punishment was, under the circumstances, an exceptionally easy one; and the Tory news-writers were not slow to suggest that he had received favourable treatment because he was a Whig author writing for a government newspaper.

Burridge was now a household word, a name used to frighten children. In his charge to the Middlesex Grand Jury in June of the same year, Whitlock Bulstrode made a pointed reference to profanity which most of his hearers no doubt understood as a comment on the Burridge case a few months before. "The sin of prophane cursing and swearing is so very great," he told them,

> and become so general amongst the common people, the soldiery and mariners, hackney-coachmen and carmen especially, that 'tis much to be feared, if there is not some stop put to it, it will draw down vengeance from Heaven upon us: No wonder that our ships so often miscarry, when our mariners curse and damn themselves through the sea to Hell. . . .

But the extent to which Burridge's awful reputation was growing may best be seen from his brief connection with the *Hanover Post-Man*. This was a weekly journal which first appeared in October, 1719; and after it had been running for a couple of months, a correspondent

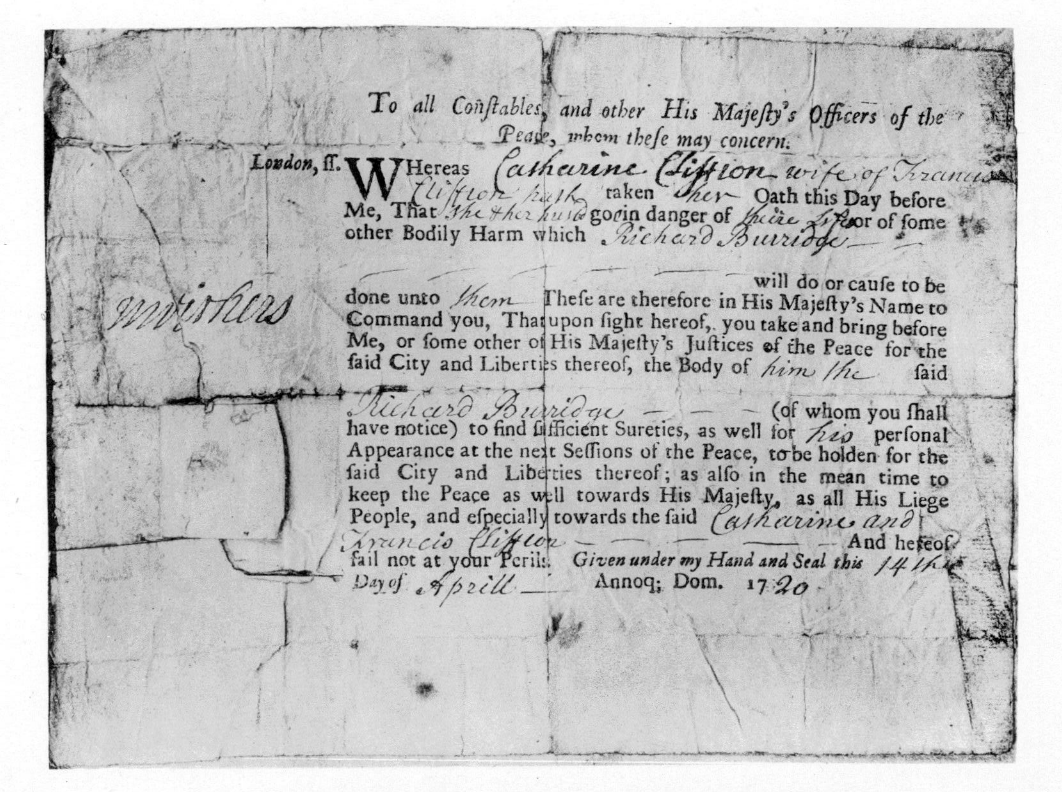

To all Conſtables, and other His Majeſty's Officers of the Peace, whom theſe may concern.

London, ſſ. WHereas Catharine Cliffton wife of Francis Cliffton hath taken her Oath this Day before Me, That she & her husb goe in danger of theire Life or of ſome other Bodily Harm which Richard Burridge — will do or cauſe to be done unto them These are therefore in His Majeſty's Name to Command you, That upon ſight hereof, you take and bring before Me, or ſome other of His Majeſty's Juſtices of the Peace for the ſaid City and Liberties thereof, the Body of him the ſaid Richard Burridge — (of whom you ſhall have notice) to find ſufficient Sureties, as well for his perſonal Appearance at the next Seſſions of the Peace, to be holden for the ſaid City and Liberties thereof; as alſo in the mean time to keep the Peace as well towards His Majeſty, as all His Liege People, and eſpecially towards the ſaid Catharine and Francis Cliffton — And hereof fail not at your Perils. *Given under my Hand and Seal this* 14th *Day of* Aprill — Annoq; Dom. 1720

A WARRANT FOR THE ARREST OF RICHARD BURRIDGE

wrote to the proprietor, Joseph Bliss, pointing out that if he wanted his paper to be a success he would have to assure his readers that it was not written by Richard Burridge, for there was a general impression in the Town that he was connected with it.

> I myself was present when a hawker was ask'd, Why she did not sell the *Hanover* Journal ; she presently replied, She thought it was a sin to sell them, because Burridge the Blasphemer writ it ; and that to her knowledge many others refused them upon the same account.

Bliss took the opportunity of printing this letter in his issue of December 19, and at the same time of speaking his mind about Burridge. He admitted that he had been foolish enough to give the man a job, but he had now got rid of him, and a good riddance it was. It appears that relations between Bliss and his author had been thoroughly unpleasant. "I doubt not," he adds, "but Burridge will go roaring and bellowing about the Town, like a madman, belching out his oaths by mouthfuls, in order (as he calls it) to damn the paper ;" but readers might rest assured that he had now no connection with it whatever. Burridge-baiting had now become a recognised sport among the news-writers, and a legitimate source of copy. When the Tory newspapers had occasion to mention him, they would sometimes print his name in heavy Gothic type ; the unfortunate man had clearly become a moral outcast. He had even grown sinister in his appearance owing to the loss of an eye. When he was writing *Religio Libertini* in 1712 he remarked that his eyes had been giving him some trouble. Constant study by the light of candles had caused violent defluxions in both eyes, and the most famous oculists and surgeons had told him that he must lose the sight of one eye altogether. They could do nothing more for him, and so Burridge decided to cure himself.

"After all their experiments try'd on me," he writes,

> I searched what physical authors I had in my study, and by conversing with the dead, found out a remedy which restor'd the most dangerous eye to sight again.

But the cure can have been no more than a temporary one, for some years later *Mist's Journal* was referring to him disrespectfully as "Monocolus."

Yet his spirit was far from being broken. Indeed, the chief attraction of Burridge is that he keeps on trying. For the next few years he is constantly in the news. He comes to the surface at short intervals like a water rat, swimming as strongly as ever, only to flop suddenly beneath the water again when some enemy throws a stone. Whatever impression Read the printer tried to give the public, it is clear that he found Burridge a useful man, for he was certainly employing him again towards the end of the year 1718. On December 27, *An Elegy upon the Death of the late King of Sweden* appeared in his *Weekly Journal,* and gave offence to the government. On being questioned about the authorship of those verses, Read named Burridge, and the blasphemer was promptly arrested. From prison he wrote to Lord Stanhope in his neat round handwriting, begging for release so that he might look after his wife and two small children.

> Yo^{r} Lordship's Petition^{r} for his unshaken'd Loyalty to ye King and Goverm^{t} hath procur'd a numerous Body of Papists, Jacobites, & other disaffected Persons to be his Enemies, insomuch that all last year they persecuted him with malicious Prosecutions, to withstand which it reduced him to great Necessities, costing him above 40*l.* besides running him above 25*l.* in Debt.

With all those extra expenses it is not surprising that Burridge should have been driven more than ever to live on his wits. On May 16, 1720, there appeared an angry advertisement in the *Daily Post* above the signature of Philip Horneck :

> Whereas an ignorant, scandalous and obscene pamphlet, entitled, Cupid restor'd to Sight, or, His Mother Venus Unveil'd, etc. has lately crept into the World with my Name prefix'd to it in the Title Page, and subscrib'd in the Dedication, I do hereby certify the Whole is a most impudent Forgery, as not being directly or indirectly concern'd in the Work, and an utter Stranger to the Publication of it.

Two days later, Samuel Redmayne, who had printed the pamphlet, offered a public apology to Horneck in the same paper, and at the same time explained what had happened. Burridge, it appears, had brought him the manuscript, and assured him that the pamphlet was Horneck's. He had printed it in good faith, but it now appeared that he had been imposed upon. No doubt Redmayne was telling the truth ; yet by this time Burridge's reputation was so scandalous that he could safely be blamed for anything.

During the greater part of 1720 he was carrying on a squabble, in and out of the law courts, with a Catholic printer, Francis Clifton. Early in May, Burridge had the satisfaction of seeing Clifton committed to Newgate on a charge of stealing his neckcloth and half a guinea out of his pocket ; but when Clifton came to stand his trial Burridge failed to appear against him, and he was discharged. Two, however, could play at this game, and Clifton was able to procure a warrant for Burridge's arrest on a charge of assault. In a letter which he wrote some months later to the Archbishop of Canterbury while he was suffering a second term of imprisonment,

Clifton has left us with some idea of what had been going on. Burridge had been molesting him continually. Last April, Clifton explains,

> he assaulted my wife, who was then bigg with child, as also my journey-man and myself standing at my own door, after which, (having not only abus'd us wth his tongue but his hands also) he broke my windows, and committed other out-rages.

After that, Burridge had trumped up his charge of robbery against him, and had him confined in Newgate. "I suppose he designs upon first opportunity to set fire to my house as he did formerly to Newgate." Meanwhile, since Clifton is not to be trusted any more than Burridge, it would be as well to consider his opponent's version of the dispute. On July 25, 1720, Burridge writes from prison to Charles Delafaye :

> This is to acquaint your Worship that I am still persecuted by y^{t} curs'd papistick, jacobite, nonjuring, highflying Party, especially one Francis Clifton, who lately assaulting and robbing me, and knowing I had a Warrant from Sir Wm. Withers to apprehend him, he, to stifle the Warrant, arrested me in an Action of 50 Pounds, tho' I owe him not a Farthing.

He suggests that Clifton should be given the Oath of Allegiance, Supremacy, and Abjuration to swear, and adds some information on his disloyal printing and his evasion of the stamp duty. On August 10, he writes again to say that he is bringing an action of £500 against Clifton, and goes on to give more information against him and against two government messengers, whom he accuses of accepting bribes. Imprisonment was bringing out the least attractive side of Burridge's wickedness. So long as he is blaspheming recklessly, setting fire to Newgate, committing assault and battery upon Clifton, and even upon Mrs. Clifton, he retains at least one's intellectual sympathy; but when he dwindles to the mere informer, the spiteful prisoner biting and scratching at all and sundry, he drops below his own high standard of wrongdoing.

As far as misdemeanours are concerned, he fades out in this rather watery sunset. There is no dying streak of blasphemy to lighten up his career in one last lurid glow; no terrible death-bed scene such as would have delighted the heart of Samuel Richardson. Burridge simply disappears from the news. Perhaps even his abundant vitality was beginning to fail him; perhaps his vicissitudes had brought him at length to a sober frame of mind. The last important event in his life seems to have been the publication in 1722 of a useful pocket guide to the streets of London. In the preface to this little work, *A New Review of London*, he tells how the compilation of it had cost him several months of continual tramping about the Town, inquiring where streets began, and where they ended, and what they were called. There one must leave him, trudging about the courts and alleys with aching feet, but not, it is to be hoped, too blasphemously, already expiating, perhaps, some part of that lengthy Purgatory that must have been in store for him.

It is a strange and unintelligent life for one who was clearly far from being a fool. "Let the day perish wherein I was born," he exclaimed in the year 1712, "and the night in which it was said, There is a man-child conceived." Most of his contemporaries would probably have echoed that with a fervent "Amen!" It was indeed no ordinary life and no commonplace wickedness that provoked the exclamation, and in a sense his wish has been granted. But even if he could be painted out of the picture completely, the age of Queen Anne would lose a thin but lurid streak of colour, and the picture would be to that slight extent impoverished. He soars like a rocket above the white, upturned faces of the scandalised multitude, climbs high in the shining track of his own wickedness, and breaks in tears of fire. A bad man, even an unpleasant man, but as a pure spectacle not unremarkable.

CURRENT INTELLIGENCE

1703–1704

Last night the only Daughter of Sir Christopher Wren was buried in St. Paul's.

On Thursday her Majesty and the Prince set out for Windsor, to continue there for the most part of the Summer.

Run away from his Master the 14th instant, Pompey a Black Boy about 15 years of Age, he had on a sad-colour'd Frock, a blue Waistcoat and blue Stockings, with a brass Collar about his Neck. . . .

On Thursday Daniel de Foe, Author of the Pamphlet, entitul'd The Shortest Way with the Dissenters, was taken, and after being examined, he was committed on Saturday to Newgate.

The Duke of Marlborough being returned to the Grand Army, a great Council of War is to be held this day or tomorrow, to consider whether the Confederate Forces are to keep the Field any longer or march into their Winter Quarters.

These are to give notice to all Gentlemen, Ladies and others, that the Great Ox that has been so long talk'd of . . . is to be seen any hour of the day, at the White Horse Inn in Fleetstreet, at the same place where the great Elephant was seen. This large and famous Beast is 19 hands high, and 4 yards long, from his Face to his Rump, and never was Calv'd nor never Suck'd. . . . This noble Beast was lately shown at the University of Cambridge, with great Satisfaction to all that saw him.

We have had so violent a Storm at South West that the like has not been known in these parts in the Memory of Man. The Light House on the Edistone off Plymouth was wash'd away, and 'tis credibly reported that Mr. Winstanely the Builder of it happen'd at that time to be in it.

The Hypochondriack Digestive Powder, a fine pleasant Medicine, which perfectly cures the deepest Melancholly and the most extream Vapours ever known in either Sex . . . to be had only at Jacob's Coffee-House in Threadneedle-street at 3s. 6d.

This day is publish'd A Sermon upon the late Dreadful Storm, Preach'd at St. Andrew's Holborn, November 28, 1703.

On Sunday night a Gentleman going from St. James's to Kensington, was met and attack'd in Hide Park by two Foot-Pads, who took from him his Sword, Watch, Perriwig and Rings, in all to the value of 130l. and left him in a deplorable Condition.

At the Bear-Garden in Hockley-in-the-Hole tomorrow being Wednesday the 22d instant, A Tryal of Skill will be perform'd between George Thattham and Francis Gorman Masters of the noble Science of Defence, for Ten Pounds, the best Man at the sharp Weapons.

Advice is come, That the 21st of July the Fleet under Sir George Rooke attack'd Gibraltar, and that it capitulated the 24th.

London, August 12. On Thursday in the Afternoon Collonel Parks, Aide de Camp to his Grace the Duke of Marlborough, arriv'd here from Germany, being sent Express, to bring an Account of a glorious Victory[1] *obtain'd over the Bavarians, by the Confederate Troops under the Command*

[1] The Battle of Blenheim.

of his Grace, the 13th instant, N.S. As my Lord Duke was in the persuit of the Enemy, he had not time to write but few Lines to my Lady Dutchess with a Lead Pencil. . . . They talk that 20 Batallions were surrounded in a village, and for the most part cut in pieces. . . . This News caus'd an universal Joy in this City, which was express'd by the fireing of the Cannon of the Tower, the ringing of Bells, Bonfires, Illuminations, etc.

A Most Excellent Plaister for the Corns, not only presently removing the anguish thereof, but likewise quite deadening them to the Root insensibly and safely, as hath been happily experienced by many. Is to be had only of Mr. Scampton at the Angel over against the Mermaid Tavern in Cornhill.

John Lacy and the Modern Prophets

Where sighs, and groans, and shrieks that rent the air,
Are made, not mark'd ; where violent sorrow seems
A modern ecstasy.

Macbeth

I

THE eighteenth century may have been the Age of Reason ; but it certainly had its irrational side. More than once in those hundred years the solid England of Queen Anne and the first four Georges trembled ominously, and all through the century there were eruptions of emotional fervour and fanaticism that indicated the streams of boiling lava beneath. If much was written and spoken against " enthusiasm " in this period, it was partly at least because men had learnt to distrust and to fear it, and not necessarily because they were insensible to the power of the emotions.

At the very beginning of the century, and among a generation which has sometimes been regarded as deplorably reasonable, there occurred a religious movement, brought over from France by a group of ecstatics known as the French Prophets, which was much queerer and more irrational than the Methodist Movement forty years later. Perhaps it could hardly be described as a movement ; it was much nearer to being an epidemic, a sort of spiritual influenza accompanied by a variety of alarming and well-marked symptoms. Those who caught the infection showed most of the familiar signs of religious hysteria, and incurred a full measure of that unpopularity which is usually the lot of the extravagantly religious. For it may be observed that if all the world loves a lover, it usually views with distaste those whose love is centred too demonstratively on their God.

The French Prophets, or Modern Prophets, as they soon came to be called, were among the most startling phenomena of the reign of Queen Anne; indeed, when their reputation was at its height they probably claimed as much of the public's attention as Marlborough and his campaigns. The sect had grown up towards the end of the seventeenth century in the mountains of the Cevennes, where the persecution of the Huguenots was particularly favourable to the growth of fanaticism. Driven out of France, several of the Prophets came to London during the winter of 1706, and joined the large body of French Protestants already settled there. They soon attracted notice by their strange agitations and contortions when under the operation of the Spirit, and by the ghastly prophetical warnings which they uttered while apparently in a state of ecstasy. Their fellow-countrymen already living in London before the Prophets came over were not impressed; they even went so far as to dissociate themselves from the new refugees by publicly declaring that their three leaders were impostors, and publishing an advertisement to that effect in the *Post Boy*. No doubt the heads of the French Church in London realised that those fanatics were not likely to be popular either with the civil or the religious authorities, and so took the discreet step of immediately disclaiming any responsibility for them. But even in the reign of Queen Anne, London was a big enough city to provide support for any cause or crusade, however fantastic; and as the months passed, and the Prophets continued to hold their queer meetings, the numbers of the new sect steadily increased. Soon it needed only a miracle of some sort to consolidate the position that they were rapidly building up for themselves, and towards the end of the year 1707 a really splendid miracle was promised to the still doubting but highly interested Londoners.

On December 23, 1707, there passed away a certain Dr. Thomas Emes. He had died as mortal men will die, the breath had left his body, and he was now decently buried in Tyndal s Burying-Ground at Bunhill Fields. "Certain, 'tis certain; very sure, very sure: death, as the Psalmist saith, is certain to all; all shall die." Dead, however, Dr. Emes was rapidly becoming a far more important person than he had ever been while merely alive. He had belonged, in fact, to this strange new sect of the French Prophets who were now disturbing London with their predictions; and as he lay upon his death-bed, several of his brother Prophets were incautious enough to comfort him with the assurance that though he was undoubtedly going to die, he would shortly be raised again like Lazarus from the dead. God was going to work a wonderful miracle upon the body of His servant Emes, to confirm the faith of His other servants and confound their enemies.

It may be that those promises were made to the dying man from the friendliest and most innocent of motives, and with no other design than to make his last hours a little easier. If that was so, the Prophets were playing with fire. Their utterances, which were always in the first person, were understood to be the voice of God Himself speaking through the lips of His servants; and therefore any promise made by one of the Prophets in a state of inspiration had to be accepted by all of them as final and irrevocable. On this occasion, however, they showed no signs of wanting to avoid the consequences of their inspiration; indeed, they proceeded to bolder and more definite predictions about Dr. Emes. On the very day that he was buried, a young prophetess declared under inspiration the name of the prophet who should perform the promised miracle:

> By the hand of my servant Lacy will I raise the body of my servant that is now dead. But you must wait my time.

All that was wanting now was a definite date for the miracle, and that was not long in coming. It was communicated at a gathering of the Prophets on New Year's Day by a certain John Potter:

> The twenty-fifth day of May, you shall behold him rise again. One month above the number of days that Lazarus was in his grave. The very hour he was put in the earth shall he arise. . . . I will by thee, [*Here he laid his hand upon J. L.'s shoulders*] raise him who shall be rotten. . . . An angelick host shall guard thee, and thy companions. No hurt shall come unto thee, nor any of mine. . . . Provide no cloathing for my servant; for he shall rise pure and innocent. Therefore no shame shall attend him. Neither shall it be esteem'd indecency for him to walk naked unto his habitation.

Finally John Lacy placed the prophecy beyond all further doubt by himself falling under the operation of the Spirit immediately after John Potter had spoken, and declaring:

> That which was said by my servant, touching the raising from the dead, shall be printed.

Printed it was a few weeks later, and all London was aware of the promised resurrection.

There was no turning back now, and the Prophets stuck bravely to their prediction. As the great day approached the excitement in London increased. Pamphlets and poems ridiculing the Prophets and their miracle kept the coffee-houses amused; sermons and tracts denouncing the new sect betrayed a certain uneasiness on the part of the Church. Many people were convinced that the Prophets were impostors, but some were not so sure, and others again were willing to be persuaded that they might after all prove genuine.

The twenty-fifth of May found the Town in a state of pleasurable commotion; it was holiday time, and the mob had been promised a new and unusual sort of entertainment. All through the afternoon a multitude of people, expectant, sceptical, or merely looking for some vulgar amusement went trailing through the streets leading to Bunhill Fields, and by six o'clock a rabble of close upon twenty thousand holiday makers was awaiting the arrival of John Lacy, who would raise this modern Lazarus from his five months' sleep among the dead. So great was the excitement that two regiments of the train-bands had been called out to prevent any disorder, and also, no doubt, to protect John Lacy and his fellow-prophets should the promised miracle fail to take place. What would have happened if the earth had suddenly parted above the grave of Dr. Emes one simply cannot imagine; but no such thing happened. Lacy and his friends merely failed to appear, and the crowds that had waited so long and so hopefully melted away in disappointment, to seek for less uncertain sources of amusement. The tombstones in Tyndal's Burying-Ground cast longer and still longer shadows, earth and sky grew dark together, and in the stiller and blacker darkness of the grave Dr. Emes slept on, unconscious of the shuffling herd of sightseers that had trampled all afternoon long above his head.

The dead are sleeping in their sepulchres :
And, mouldering as they sleep, a thrilling sound,
Half sense, half thought, among the darkness stirs . . .

II

When the French Prophets first came to London they had few friends and little money ; but it was not long before they found two English allies, who were both men of some standing, and—what was perhaps more important—of considerable substance. One of those was certainly a fool ; the other cannot be so easily dismissed. The fool was Sir Richard Bulkeley, a tiny deformed baronet with a quite pathetic faith in everything he heard or saw, the sort of man that one would like to have in the audience if one were performing a particularly difficult conjuring trick. Sir Richard may have been astute enough in some matters, but in everything connected with the Prophets he was entirely credulous. If one of them had told him that he would shortly become Queen Anne's second husband, or that St. Paul's Cathedral would suddenly rise and float away to Wapping, he would not have doubted it ; for there was no limit to his faith, and he had already believed far stranger things than those. It was observed that he was going about in a very shabby suit of clothes, not at all becoming a wealthy baronet ; but Sir Richard had a good reason for not renewing his clothes just yet. It had been revealed to him that through His Servant, John Lacy, God would effect a miraculous cure of his deformity ; and Sir Richard, who fully believed that his crooked back would be made straight, saw no sense in ordering his tailor to make him a suit of clothes that would only have to be thrown aside when he was cured.

He seems not to have had visions or agitations himself; but his credulity and enthusiasm supplied just that kind of warm, encouraging atmosphere in which the Prophets could function most successfully. Sir Richard was always there in a corner of the room, lending authority by his rank, and moral support by his unconcealed admiration for those whom he quite honestly believed to be the chosen mouthpieces of God. Frequently, too, he proved himself highly useful by translating prophetic utterances for the benefit of those who knew no French; for it was to be observed that when the Spirit spoke through the lips of a French-born prophet the message was always in French, even though everyone else in the room was English. On such occasions Sir Richard would oblige, acting as a sort of middle man to the middle men. Most important of all, he was reputed to be worth £30,000, and it is probable that a good part of the Prophets' expenses was met by large advances from his pocket. No doubt the money was well enough invested; the Prophets had given him a new interest in life, and were brightening his last years with a strange, painful excitement, which to old gentlemen of deadened faculties is the nearest approach to the joys of green and lusty youth.

The other important person who threw in his lot with the French Prophets in London was John Lacy, a gentleman said to be worth at one time £2,000 a year. Unlike Sir Richard, he was in the prime of life—in his forty-second year—when the Prophets came over, and before long he managed, by the force of his personality and by the influence that his wealth and position gave him, to secure a commanding position among them. He was a non-conformist, and a leading member of Dr. Edmund Calamy's congregation at Westminster; he had, indeed, been the first to sign the call that brought Dr. Calamy to that important charge. He was, moreover, a married man with a family; one, in fact, who appeared to be anchored securely to respectability and the pious commonplaces of a decent and regular religion. But the coming of the Prophets seems to have awakened some sleeping passion in the mind of Lacy, and to have suggested to him the possibility of a religious experience much more exciting than any that the Rev. Dr. Calamy had been able to provide, or would have cared to encourage.

He began attending the meetings of the Prophets in the winter of 1706, and there he would watch their strange agitations; he seized every opportunity of conversing with them, and of questioning their followers. For some time he seems to have remained no more than a spectator, but beneath the surface strange forces were already at work. Something was going wrong with Lacy; he grew moody, and began to act in a queer way. Mrs. Lacy, a decent, sensible woman by all accounts, found herself more and more neglected, and not for another woman, or the pleasures of the tavern. Like Shakespeare's Brutus, her husband had simply withdrawn into himself; he spent his days staring into vacancy, and brooding over a secret which he apparently found it impossible to share with her. Plain, sensible Dr. Calamy was inclined to blame a vexatious lawsuit for his moody state of mind; but Lacy was clearly going through some kind of spiritual crisis. He was now preparing for publication a series of prophetical warnings uttered by the French Prophets. Dr. Calamy urged him to be careful of what he was doing, but his advice was disregarded. At last the inevitable happened: one morning Lacy woke in his bed to find himself in a state of agitation. His breath began to come faster and faster, and his head started to shake horizontally from side to side. This was followed by twitchings in the stomach (" not much unlike an hyccop "), and a choking sensation in the windpipe. In later agitations his hands and arms were often shaken violently, and sometimes there were catchings and twitches all over his body. These were the outward signs ; but along with the visible agitation there went a spiritual joy, an elevation of soul that more than compensated for any physical inconvenience he might have to endure. As yet, however, he had not himself begun to utter prophecies.

Life was now becoming very difficult for poor Mrs. Lacy, who saw her husband apparently going out of his mind, and was yet quite unable to help him. Before long he had sunk into a state of dejection, refusing to eat and drink, and scarcely taking any notice of her when they happened to be together. In despair she wrote a letter to Dr. Calamy, inviting him to come to dinner but suggesting that he should pretend to her husband that he had just dropped in accidentally. Dr. Calamy fell in with this innocent conspiracy, and duly presented himself at the Lacy's house, where he found his host a sadly altered man. The lawsuit had now been settled —it had gone against him—and he was quite unable to sleep. Dr. Calamy, acting apparently from a sense of duty, informed Lacy that he had been told his cause was not a very good one, and Lacy lost his temper. The pastoral visit was not, in fact, a success. Some time later he became delirious, and had to be confined in a dark room. He recovered, but though he still attended Dr. Calamy's church he still kept in touch with the Prophets. Mrs. Lacy, who saw things going steadily from bad to worse, now blamed Calamy for not having taken a firmer line with her husband ; after all, he was responsible for Mr. Lacy's soul, and he had allowed it to get into this alarming condition. Stung by this criticism, Calamy proceeded to preach a series of sermons from his own pulpit against the new Prophets, and Lacy sat in his pew and listened to them.

Soon, however, events began to move much faster. One day when Dr. Calamy was dining again with the family, an event occurred which must have told him that he had already lost the battle. In the middle of dinner Lacy suddenly rose to his feet, gripped the table as if to prevent himself from falling, and proceeded without a word of apology or explanation to walk upstairs. To Mrs. Lacy this sort of conduct was now a commonplace; she explained to her minister that Lacy was just about to go into one of his agitations, and added significantly that she believed he would like Dr. Calamy to look on while they were in progress. How, it may be asked, did she know that her husband would like Dr. Calamy to look on? Had Lacy said as much to her? Or did she perhaps suspect that the whole thing was an elaborate fraud, and that her husband only wanted to stage an impressive exhibition in front of his own minister? Calamy, at any rate, went on to finish his dinner; he was made of solid and imperturbable stuff, and no doubt Mrs. Lacy found comfort in his phlegmatic calm after her husband's moody and agitated ways. When at length Calamy had made an end, he asked Mrs. Lacy if there was any place where he might watch her husband without being observed. There was; she took him upstairs to a closet with a glass door, through which he had a good view of the adjoining room. "I went," says Calamy, "as softly as I could to this glass door, and stood there a great while, and saw him seated upon an easy chair by the bed-side, with his back towards me, heaving to and fro ; and heard a humming noise, but no sound that was at all distinct. I asked Mrs. Lacy whether that was all I was like to see and hear. She told me she believed I could expect no more, continuing there ; but she was satisfied he expected I would come in to him, and then she doubted not but I should see and hear more." Again the suggestion that her husband was play-acting, that he was only waiting for his audience before he began to prophecy.

Dr. Calamy went in, however, and took Lacy by the hand. When he let the hand drop again, it fell flat on his knees. All this time Lacy appeared to be unconscious that there was anyone else in the room ; he was still humming away, and gradually the sound grew louder, and the heaving in his breast increased, until the agitations reached his throat and it almost seemed as if he would be suffocated. And then at last he began to speak. He spoke in single syllables, with a heave and breath between each syllable.

> Thou hast been my faithful servant ; and I have honoured thee. But I do not take it well that thou slightest and opposest my servants and messengers. If thou wilt fall in with these my servants, thou shalt do great things in this dispensation ; and I will use thee as a glorious instrument to my praise, and I will take care of thee and thine. But if thou goest on to oppose my servants, thou wilt fall under my severe displeasure.

This utterance of the Spirit, directed apparently against Dr. Calamy, seemed to relieve Lacy, for the humming gradually abated. At length he rose up, shook himself, and rubbed his eyes as if he had just wakened from sleep. . . . A little too much emphasis here, perhaps ? "Where am I ? Heigh, ho ! Have I been asleep ?" One can almost see Mrs. Lacy exchanging a quick glance with Dr. Calamy ; and whatever evidence of abnormal spiritual experience there may be in Lacy's subsequent career with the Prophets this particular episode is surely quite bogus. Dr. Calamy, at any rate, was entirely sceptical. Lacy went back to his dinner, declaring that he had no recollection of what he had said or done in the interval. A little later he said that he believed he was going to have another fit. "But I told him," says Dr. Calamy, who clearly looked on Lacy and his fits as a child with a new toy, "I was fully satisfied with what I had seen and heard, and so took my leave."

III

Lacy was now beyond the aid of his minister; and for the future Calamy contented himself with offering prayers for the recovery of his sanity, and with endeavouring to prevent this strange religious epidemic, this *morbus Gallicus* of the soul, from spreading to others. He delivered two lectures at Salter's Hall against the Prophets, and published them with the title of *A Caveat against New Prophets,* and a dedication to Lacy, who afterwards complained of Calamy's impertinence in sympathising publicly with his wife ("your pious comfort") and his children ("your agreeable offspring"). Sir Richard Bulkeley replied to the *Caveat* on behalf of the Prophets, and Calamy answered his reply. The Prophets had begun as a topic of conversation; they were now achieving the dignity of a controversy. Before long a considerable literature had grown up around them: on the one side, their own printed prophecies, their vindications and answers, and on the other, caveats, criticisms, sermons, satires, exposures, poems, and plays. At the theatrical booths in Smithfield Fair the agitations of the Prophets were acted in pantomime ; at the other end of the Town there was Durfey's comedy, *The Modern Prophets*, in which pretty Mistress Bignall delighted the sparks by going off into dainty little agitations on the stage. Indeed, at no time could the Prophets complain of neglect ; if they wanted notoriety—and some of them probably wished for little else—they had certainly got it.

Their agitations were undoubtedly responsible for much of the interest they aroused. They were continually going into convulsions ; groaning, gasping, humming, sighing, sobbing, hiccupping, gulping, grimacing, and even at times whistling and dancing. It was not uncommon, too, when the prophetic fit came on, for one of the inspired to be flung violently upon the floor, or to crash against a chair or table. The Spirit worked in different ways, and individual prophets had their own peculiar form of response to it. John Cavalier, for instance, one of the original Prophets from France, used to walk on his hands, with his legs erect, and in that unusual posture to utter his prophetic warnings. But the generally accepted procedure was for the Prophet at the approach of inspiration to be seized with an involuntary shaking and trembling, not unlike St. Vitus' dance or those agitations which were commonly attributed to the earliest Quakers. Sir Richard Bulkeley, who had witnessed many strange sights among the Prophets, such as men " falling backward at once, and without the least bending of the ham, so that the scull has come to the floor as soon as any other part of the body whatsoever," has left a very precise and circumstantial account of their agitations :

They generally begin in the limbs, and then affect the lungs by a vibration of breathing, in some so quick as, in the measure of time, may be four in a second, or in musick, in slow common

> time, a semiquaver. Then some find great vibrations of the head ; with some it is forwards and backwards, or from before to behind ; with others it is with an horizontal motion as a dog that turns his head when he comes out of the water : then there comes an involuntary motion of the tongue, that as they walk in the streets they find their tongue moving in the mouth as if it would speak.

When the agitations had reached a sufficient height, the prophet would begin to articulate. As the words poured from his lips, or crept forth in separate gasps, a scribe with pen, ink, and paper would be busily writing them down. No sooner had one prophet returned to his normal self than another was apt to show signs of inspiration ; indeed, at any gathering of the Prophets several of them might be prophesying at the same time, for the inspiration was undoubtedly epidemic.

Along with the actual prophecy went a considerable amount of miming. Lacy in particular seems to have been led by the Spirit to act the very warnings that were issuing from his lips ; his various gestures were faithfully observed by the scribes, and added in marginal notes to his printed prophecies. On Thursday, July 8, 1707, for instance, he uttered the following prophetic warning under the influence of the Spirit :

> The harvest is at hand. The sickle is already put in to gather it : and I will thresh all nations. The chaff, and straw, and all refuse shall be purged away : The good grain alone remain upon the earth.

The faithful scribe took it all down, but he has also preserved for posterity the very gestures of the prophet :

> *At the beginning of this inspiration he rose up, and with his arms he laid about him like a man, threshing for above* 20 *strokes.*

On other occasions Lacy imitated a trumpet, a drum, the tolling of a bell, and sometimes several of the Prophets would be performing together what was almost a miniature play.

Meanwhile the Town looked on with mixed feelings. Of those who had no belief in the Prophets at all, some were charitable enough to hold that they were the victims of a peculiarly dangerous form of religious hysteria. One impressionable young man who attended several of their meetings found that he could not watch the Prophets in their agitations without himself beginning to twitch; even to think of them when alone was sometimes enough to set him off into what he calls "irregular motions." The nerves, as he very properly remarks, "are affected withal when we behold a person yawning, to imitate the motion we see in another."

Many of the powers claimed by mediums in the twentieth century, such as automatic writing, clairvoyance, and levitation, were apparently to be found among the members of this sect more than two hundred years ago. Sir Richard had even seen some of them plunge their hands into burning coal. Unfortunately the evidence for their possession of abnormal powers rests almost entirely upon their own unsupported statements, or upon the testimony of credulous and biased witnesses, and there is not, therefore, any means of determining whether or not the Prophets ever produced what in a scientific laboratory would be regarded as genuine psychic phenomena. What is now a commonplace to the student of morbid psychology, and even to the man in the street, might easily seem astonishing or even miraculous to the men and women of 1708; though one or two of the clergymen who attacked the Prophets in sermon or pamphlet were, in fact, able to refer with some show of learning to similar phenomena in the ancient world.

Others, again, who were willing to admit that the Prophets might be controlled by some spirit, pointed out, shrewdly enough, that it had still to be proved that this Spirit came from God and not from the Evil One. As one orthodox critic put it: "God, I think, is offended, that when His gracious and good Spirit descended down on Christ as a dove, these here shou'd be for bringing Him down as a vulture, to tear and shake them in pieces in the communication of it to them." And, of course, there were plenty of downright people then as now to whom the whole affair was ridiculously simple; the Modern Prophets were merely impostors, cunning enough to play upon the credulity of such wealthy dupes as Sir Richard Bulkeley. Yet when one has to deal with a body of religious enthusiasts drawn from all classes of society and from most forms of religion or irreligion, it is wise to suspect the simplest explanation, or indeed any explanation that attempts to reduce them to a single formula. By the beginning of 1708 their numbers had grown to about two hundred, and they were increasing every week. In a large body such as this, it is probable that though many may have been rogues and hypocrites, others were almost certainly genuine; they were not, in fact, conscientiously deceiving themselves or others, and they may have been producing just those abnormal phenomena which interest the psychic investigator today. About the leaders of the Modern Prophets it is possible to have grave doubts; but among the rank and file there were undoubtedly many simple souls who had been caught up on the edge of a momentary whirlwind, and were being twirled about by a force over which they had no control. And the problem is even more complicated still; for among the twitching and groaning and stampeding crowd of the Prophets and their followers, there were probably some who were only half-convinced, willing to let themselves be swept away by mass suggestion and yet clinging obstinately to common sense: wet and clammy leaves that would gladly go sailing into the troubled air, but that only succeed in blowing damply along the ground.

But surely it would have been possible to prove the Prophets false by an appeal to their own predictions, for many of those had failed? Yes, but apparently some of them had come off. Jerusalem may have stoned her Prophets, but among Aryans there has always been a marked tendency to be strongly impressed by a successful prophecy. "If," as Voltaire noticed, "but one of the hundred events which impostors dare to predict come to pass, all the others are forgotten, and it is recorded as a token of God's favour and evidence of a prodigy. If a prediction is not fulfilled, it is explained away and a new meaning given to it." It was, in fact, by no means so easy to expose the Modern Prophets as many of their opponents had supposed. From the first they showed a quite remarkable ingenuity in answering their critics; indeed, they had all that subtlety of argument which is so frequently found adorning a bad cause. To those who pointed out that their agitations, and for that matter their general behaviour, seemed most unlike what one would expect from men of God, they replied with some show of reason that His ways were inscrutable. There were plenty of scoffers, of course; but there were many, too, who hardly dared to be so positive, "not knowing," as one of them put it, "but that God, whose ways are in the deep . . . might in this latter day reveal Himself in an extraordinary manner, for some extraordinary end." Why not, indeed? It was all rather alarming, and all very queer.

If you came to think of it, Jesus Christ was only a carpenter's son: the Jews had been expecting something much grander than that. Sir Richard, too, struck several shrewd blows for the Prophets. They claimed that they were performing miraculous cures, and in many quarters it was suggested that those miracles were simply ingenious tricks. To Sir Richard the answer was obvious: "The Pharisees believ'd that the raising of Lazarus was but a poor plot between him and our Saviour." There was no arguing with the Prophets and their apologists; they could be refuted only by time, and until the repeated failure of their predictions began to tell against them they made a brave stand for it. Even when they had been driven into a corner by the failure of Lacy to raise Dr. Emes from the dead, they brought forward the most surprising and ingenious explanations to account for that.

The major prophet, the acknowledged head of the whole sect, was undoubtedly Lacy. In technique, as Dr. Calamy and others have noted, his prophesying was extremely slow; he paused between each syllable "just like children learning their primmer." Some of the other Prophets had a much more rapid flow of utterance; and Lacy's slow tempo, however welcome it must have been to the scribes who had to take the sacred words down, laid him open to the sneers of sceptical onlookers, who saw in his want of fluency only the halting performance of an immature actor. On one occasion, too, if we are to believe an unfriendly witness, he committed a serious breach of prophetic etiquette. It was, of course, understood that when a Prophet was under the operation of the Spirit he was completely unconscious of his surroundings, and was in fact transported out of himself. In the summer of 1707, shortly after he had joined the Prophets, Lacy was seen by this observer under the operation of the Spirit, and so violent were his agitations that he shook off his wig. No gentleman in 1707 worth £2000 a year would care to be seen in mixed company without his wig, and it appears that Lacy—without interruption to his agitations—felt for the wig and cleverly replaced it on his head. This is not quite what one would have expected, but then perhaps one would hardly expect to find a Prophet in a peruke.

His first prophetical warning came to him in the month of June, 1707. By the beginning of August he was performing miracles through the Spirit, or so he let it be known. The public was informed that on August 4 he had cured a young prophetess, Betty Gray, of her blindness, by stroking her eyes three times with his thumbs. It should be remarked that the girl had been blind only a few hours when Lacy worked his miraculous cure; there had never been anything wrong with her eyesight until on that particular day she suddenly got up from the dinner table, clapped her hands over her eyes, and cried that she could no longer see. Sir Richard had no doubt that she had really been struck blind; he could see her eyes for himself, and they were "flaccid and undulating."

Betty Gray soon became famous. The niece of a candle snuffer at one of the theatres, she had run away from home to join the Prophets, and before long she was going into ecstasies with the best of them. She appears to have been a young woman of high spirits—"a wild skittish girl," she is called by one commentator—and she undoubtedly possessed great physical energy. Not content with restoring her sight, Lacy went on to announce that on Sunday, August 17, he would perform

QUEEN ANNE PLAYING-CARDS (I)

a second miracle upon her body. It had been revealed to him by the Spirit that there would appear in her throat a hard excrescence of flesh, or bone, which would make her neck swell and so choke her ; she would be brought to the point of death, but would be saved by the operation of the Spirit. Happily for posterity, the curiosity of a certain Quaker had been excited by the Prophets. He was present at their meeting on the night of August 17, watched the proceedings with dispassionate interest, and afterwards wrote an account of what he had seen. He may, of course, have been a biased spectator, willing to put the worst possible construction upon everything he saw on that Sunday night ; but it must be admitted that the whole business had a very odd appearance. Was the girl going to become desperately ill just to allow Lacy to cure her ? Could it be that Betty Gray, this wild, skittish young woman from the Playhouse, had learnt to do the same alarming things —first with her eyeballs and now with her thorax— that other people can do with double-jointed fingers ? At all events we must make what we can of the Quaker's story, for it is the best we have. When he entered the room where the Prophets were meeting, the girl was already in full agitation ; head, hands, and body were all shaking violently, and a choking noise was coming from her throat. Her chin was pressed firmly against her neck as if she were trying to stop her breath, and before long she began to look " bloted and black in the face." At length she started to crawl on her knees all round the room, until finally she came to Lacy's chair ; there she stopped, and " placed her head in Esquire Lacy's lap." Lacy now asked those who were present to come and feel her neck. Was it not very hard ? Some thought it was, but others were doubtful ; and the outraged Quaker had to look on while the young woman "prostituted her neck and breasts to be felt by everyone there present." Apparently her neck was not yet hard enough to satisfy the doubting Thomases in the company, for she now returned to her chair and went through fresh convulsions. After some time she was felt again, and it was generally agreed that the neck was now considerably harder ; but there was still some doubt as to whether you could honestly say that there was a bone there yet. It was at this point, according to the Quaker, that a certain John Davis spoilt everything by officiously performing the miracle himself. More curious than the rest, or more sceptical, he forcibly lifted up the girl's chin from her bosom—"which was no sooner done, but her neck felt as soft and well as ever it was ; but immediately upon his letting her go, and her putting her chin again in the same place, her neck return'd to be as hard as before." This unexpected turn of events reduced the meeting to confusion, and a number of people openly complained that the whole thing was a cheat. It was suggested on behalf of the Prophets that the Spirit must have willed it otherwise, and Lacy, as if to turn defence into attack, was suddenly seized with prophetic agitations and denounced woes from Heaven on all who had opposed the miracle. The warnings uttered on this occasion have been preserved for us by Lacy himself ; and when it is remembered that the Prophet is not supposed to be speaking his own thoughts but faithfully pronouncing the commands of the Spirit, the words have a very queer appearance indeed. Here, at any rate, is the message that broke from the lips of the Prophet :

> If any one believes an assembly to be deluded, he has no right to disturb others who do in faith attend. Here I further declare,

> that I will exercise the rod of my vengeance upon those that shall openly vilify, provoke and blaspheme where others are met to hear my servants as the messengers of God. I will not leave their embassy long without the proof of the authority of him whom they represent. How can any of you know that the person before you did of her self counterfeit the strangling? Presumption is the most: but to build upon a presumption is not wisdom in any thing. . . . Nevertheless be it known to you, my servant did not counterfeit that which you saw: nor will I suffer any of my messengers to counterfeit.

One may perhaps be forgiven for suggesting that the Spirit seems here to be stooping to mere argument, and a querulous sort of argument at that. The evening had not been a success.

In the course of the next few months Lacy laid claim to several more miraculous cures, performed (as he said) by the operation of the Spirit. A certain Mr. Preston had a terrible carbuncle on the nape of his neck, about five inches in diameter; and it was revealed to Lacy that he must cure this man. He solemnly pronounced the words, "I command away the tumour," and in ten days it had disappeared. Similarly, an old man of seventy-two was restored to sight, a child was relieved of a fever, and Sir Joseph Tyley was cured of the gout in his stomach. True or false, however, none of these miracles was sufficiently spectacular to awaken much belief in a generation that was accustomed to quacks of every sort, and they further suffered from being performed in private. If Lacy had been able to make Sir Richard's crooked little body straight—still more if he had done so before a multitude of people—that would have been something worth talking about; but the old baronet remained, for all his faith, incurably twisted to the very end. Sir Richard did, however, benefit very remarkably from his association with the Prophets.

All his life he had been an invalid, dieting, purging, and taking care of himself in a hundred little ways. "Now," he was able to write in 1708, "I live out of regimen, and live like other men; I sit up reading frequently till two, sometimes three a clock in the morning; I sup at eleven at night, or after, and upon any thing, even flesh-meat, and that hot or cold, and with beer, ale or wine; and yet do, after it, rise every morning fresh and well, after five hours, but frequently after fewer hours rest. All Glory be to God." But if this startling change was a sufficient miracle to Sir Richard, it was hardly picturesque enough to appeal to the popular imagination. The mob wanted something that they could see; they looked for an immediate and present demonstration of miraculous powers. They pressed round the Prophets asking absurd questions: "Tell me how much money I have in my pocket," or "Tell me what I was thinking yesterday." That would be a real miracle, if the Prophets could answer such a question; that would be worth something. Or if Lacy had fulfilled his prophecy that he would walk upon fire, that would have been more satisfactory than the curing half a dozen boils, or the gout, or a baronet's dyspepsia. "I know a person," wrote one of the scoffers, "that offers to defray the charge of wood and coals, if Mr. Lacy will be pleas'd to put it into the *Gazette*, or into any other printed publick paper, the certain day and hour when he will make this tryal in Smithfield; and there he will not fail of finding a fire ready lighted." Mr. Lacy declined, however, to turn himself into a public exhibition to amuse a holiday crowd at Smithfield Fair.

The miracles, indeed, fell quite flat with the public. What had much more effect on the minds of the credulous was Lacy's alarming prophecies of impending disasters.

Here, again, although almost all sensible men were sceptical, there was always the one chance in a thousand that the Prophets might be right after all. They were certainly threatening enough. Famine and pestilence, fire and brimstone were all promised to London within a few short months. Believers were commanded by the Spirit to lay in a stock of provisions to last for six months, for there would come a terrible famine; some of the inspired even had visions of people dropping down dead in the streets of starvation, or howling fearfully in the last torments of hunger. At least one old lady attended to those warnings, and (as her son tells us) laid in a stock of meal, peas, salted beef, pork, raisins, and red herrings. On March 25, 1708, fire and brimstone were to pour down on London and consume the wicked, and so numerous were the wicked that there would not be enough men left alive to bury the dead. Not content with those more or less traditional warnings, some of the inspired had visions of a still more startling kind. The Prophets should walk over their shoes in the blood of their enemies. . . . One of their number even saw a boat sailing along the streets on the blood of the slain. It was prophesied of Lord Chief Justice Holt (who had sentenced several Prophets to the pillory in 1707) that while he was sitting on the bench the blood would suddenly burst out of his veins from head to foot. Such prophecies were offensive to some, and alarming to others; but they had such an orthodox scriptural ring that many timid souls felt they must be true. Perhaps, too, evangelists always fill their ranks most successfully, not when they entreat you to come in, but when they threaten you with what will happen if you stay out.

On the great majority of Queen Anne's subjects, however, such denunciations had only the effect of making the Prophets unpopular. No one likes to be told that he is going to be burnt, or drowned, or struck with a thunderbolt, while those who are promising him those things are to be saved. Such a prediction implies a particularly offensive sort of superiority on the part of the prophet, all the more distasteful because it is quite unanswerable. There is evidence to show that the Prophets came in for a good deal of rough handling from the mob. When their meetings were open to the public, a party of unbelievers and blasphemers was apt to arrive, looking for the same sort of entertainment as they would get from a half-wit or a drunk woman. One after another of Lacy's printed prophecies is accompanied by an ominous marginal note: "*This was spoken at a public meeting where there was a great disturbance.*" On such occasions as those, the awful doom prophesied for interrupters can only have been a fresh source of delight to the irreligious. Sometimes, indeed, the meetings ended in complete uproar. Sir Richard writes sadly of an occasion when a mob broke into the meeting-house at the Barbican, rode about the hall on horseback, winding a horn and beating a drum, shouting, bellowing, throwing stones and dirt, and insulting the Prophets both male and female. Lacy mentions other occasions when the Prophets, warned by the Spirit that their enemies were at hand, managed to escape in the nick of time. All this, of course, was only to be expected in the first decade of the eighteenth century. Breaking up or setting fire to the meeting-houses of Dissenters was one of the major amusements of the period, and to the London mob Lacy and his friends were only a peculiarly unpleasant tribe of the Dissenting race. They made things still more unpleasant for themselves by wearing strips of green ribbon about a yard long, as a mark for the avenging angel to know them by when he should come to destroy the wicked. No doubt, too, this pathetic yard of ribbon served as a kind of uniform or embryonic shirt, giving to the little body a sense of exclusiveness, of being themselves the excluders, and not (as indeed they were) the excluded.

In another quarter, too, the Prophets had raised up for themselves a host of enemies. From the very beginning the Church had viewed them with grave distaste, and before long it became really hostile. Any movement such as that of the Prophets must be in some degree a criticism of existing religious institutions. Lacy was always careful to maintain that he was perfectly orthodox in his beliefs, and was only supplementing the work of revealed religion, but the clergy soon saw how the utterances of Lacy and his followers might be levelled at the Church. The Prophets with their new and imaginary authority were trying to make Christians dissatisfied with the ordinary revelation of God through the Scriptures, and so bringing contempt on His Church. It was the Church's job to save men's souls, and the Prophets really implied that it was not working fast enough. Lacy went further, and (under the operation of the Spirit) referred to the clergy as "soul-brokers," men who preached for hire. Soon the Prophets were being attacked from all sections of the Church in sermon and treatise, but this only provoked them to retaliate in the form of more prophetic warnings. The Church, however, was a formidable opponent; its ministers were educated men, well trained in an age of religious controversy to deliver shrewd and unsparing blows. Lacy, for instance, had taken to prophesying in Latin. It was held among the Prophets that this was an infallible sign that the words spoken came from God;

they could not possibly come from Lacy himself, since on his own admission he knew no more Latin than the little he had picked up at school almost thirty years ago. The clergy, however, had their answer to that. They quoted some of the Latin prophecies (pointing out incidentally how strange it was that God should choose this language to make His will known to Englishmen), and showed that they were in fact expressed in the most wretched dog Latin. Even if God were likely to speak through the mouth of His prophet in Latin, was it likely to be Latin " such as a schoolboy ought to be whipt for " ? This was clearly a point for the clergymen, and one that Lacy never answered satisfactorily. Besides this rather scholarly sort of criticism, he had to meet numerous charges of immorality made against him and his followers. There were love-feasts and orgies of various kinds ; and Betty Gray was not above suspicion. To all such accusations Lacy gave an emphatic denial ; but what men are anxious to believe they will not willingly disbelieve, and the rumours persisted. There is, in fact, considerable evidence to show that some of the Prophets were either thoroughly debauched, or else too crazed in their wits to be responsible for what they did. One old woman, known among the sect as " The Perpetual Spring," behaved habitually in so lewd a manner that one can only assume she was a sort of exhibitionist ; and there must have been many hysterical and mentally unstable creatures among Lacy's disciples upon whom the sight of others in their agitations had a highly disturbing effect.

IV

Ridiculed, denounced, man-handled, threatened with prosecution, the Prophets continued for some time to gain ground in London. If faith were enough, they must have carried everything before them. It is clear what was happening. To every fresh proselyte there came a new and thrilling sense of importance, a sense of having been singled out by God to do His work. Some fascinated young man, hanging back doubtfully at a meeting of the Prophets, would suddenly find one of the inspired standing over him in a state of ecstasy and addressing him in words that came apparently direct from God Himself. A hand would be laid on his head, and the blessed words spoken. The young prophet would be told that he had been chosen, and that the Lord would make him a pillar in His temple. One had to be very strong or very sceptical to resist this sort of thing. Samuel Keimer, a young printer who experienced this laying on of hands and received his call, has described his feelings on that occasion: "I was willing, with a sort of hope . . . to believe that it was God spoke to me." On the other hand, he was afraid it might be the Devil; but above all he was flattered and excited that he had been singled out. Was it really true that God had noticed him particularly—Samuel Keimer, the young apprentice printer? In later years Keimer was quite convinced that it was not true; but he managed to believe at the time because he was so desperately anxious to be persuaded. He was now one of the elect, with all the fierce satisfaction that such a situation can give. Keimer was willing to admit that the Prophets had a quite extraordinary hold over him at one time. Had he been commanded by them to kill his own father and mother, "or even the late Queen on the throne," he believed that he would at least have tried it. And the Prophets had another hold over the minds of their followers; they kept them in fear. "Do not mock," a woman whispered earnestly at a meeting of the Prophets to a clergyman who was inclined to be scornful: "God will strike thee dumb."

The movement reached its height in the early months of 1708. By warnings and prophecies of a general kind the Prophets had managed to preserve their reputation, but now they had staked all on the promised resurrection of Dr. Emes. It was to be no hole and corner business this time; the miracle was to be performed by John Lacy in broad daylight before as many people as cared to come and look. And finally Sir Richard Bulkeley had admitted that this miracle was to be regarded as decisive; if it failed he would agree that the Prophets were impostors. "Hold them to the point," Daniel Defoe urged the readers of his *Review*; "it was their own offer that if this did not come to pass they would own they were deluded." It is worth pausing here to ask why the Prophets had been so rash as to leave themselves no possibility of retreat. Were they willing to accept ultimate ridicule and exposure for the sake of five glorious months of notoriety? Certainly the promised raising of Dr. Emes was the best advertisement they could have given themselves. Had they, then, simply decided to spend the public's credulity like prodigals, and to enjoy while they might the publicity that the dead man was giving them? To anyone who believes that they were mere frauds this is perhaps the only possible explanation. Nor is it difficult to see how the situation may have got out of hand. The Prophets were essentially individualists, uttering their warnings and predictions as the Spirit moved them ; if they were true Prophets they would presumably, however numerous they might be, all bear the same sort of testimony. But if they were, in fact, cheats, the staff work required to ensure that their prophecies were not contradictory, or—what is even worse—impossible, must have been extraordinarily difficult. In theory, at any rate, any utterance in a state of inspiration came direct from God, and once it had been made it had to be accepted, whatever complications it might give rise to, and however awkward it might prove. Perhaps some of the minor prophets lost their heads over Dr. Emes, and forced an issue upon Lacy which he would gladly have avoided.

If that is so, Lacy certainly faced his troubles with a brave heart. As late as April 29, 1708, less than a month before the promised miracle, he was writing confidently about the event. "I did rejoice when the six months was prescrib'd, and I do the same now at the approach of the 25th of May, without the least weight upon my Spirits about the event of it. None, I am sure, can discern any upon me, nor do I find it within my self." The truth about Lacy is probably to be found in the simple, if startling, explanation that he did, in fact, believe—or, at any rate, hope—that he would be given power to raise the dead man from his grave. When one thinks of the conditions usually demanded by the twentieth-century medium—darkness or semi-darkness, joined hands in a circle, talking or singing or playing a gramophone, or all three together—before a gauze handkerchief rises a few feet above the table, one can only marvel at Lacy's apparent confidence in his power to perform a much more difficult sort of raising, and that too in the brutal daylight. It must be remembered that the Prophets were continually wrought up into a state of spiritual epilepsy ; if Lacy was not literally inspired, he was at all events frequently beside himself. All through those exciting months of 1707 he had been living a quite abnormal life, the unsteady nucleus of a whirling spiritual nebula. He had cut himself adrift from his old regular life, and was flying before the gusts of a storm that he did not even attempt to control. Men, of course, will often do much for the sake of notoriety, and to one hungering for notice it is better, perhaps, to be laughed at or despised than merely to be ignored ; but Lacy's mental aberrations can hardly be explained away in such terms as those. Whatever his original motives for joining the Prophets, it seems clear that he came in time to believe in himself as one divinely inspired ; and no doubt the raising of Dr. Emes, though a stiff task for a Prophet, did not seem to him beyond his powers. One may even suppose that he knelt down quite innocently and prayed that he might be given faith enough to perform the miracle. But what a situation for a man to find himself in ! No wonder that when the 25th of May came round Lacy realised that the task was too much for him, and prudently stayed at home.

The failure to resurrect Dr. Emes was the beginning of the end. Sure enough, Lacy was ready with his explanations and his excuses, which he published at full in *Esquire Lacy's Reasons why Dr. Emes was not Raised from the Dead ;* but the public had been cheated of its promised entertainment, and it never forgave the Prophets. From now onwards they did most of their prophesying in the provincial towns, where they made themselves a nuisance to the local magistrates. In the course of the next two years they visited such large cities as Bristol, Coventry, Worcester, Oxford, Cambridge,

Edinburgh and Glasgow (from both of which they were driven out by order of the magistrates), and they penetrated even to Ireland, Wales, and Holland. Prophecy is best combined with an itinerant life; you can be over the hills and far away long before your predictions are due to take place, and it is usually as well that you can.

V

The closing phases of this odd movement are in some ways the oddest of all. Schisms began to appear among the ranks of the Prophets. The most serious rebel was Sir Richard Bulkeley, who did not apparently lose faith in prophecy, but who may possibly have lost faith in Lacy. At all events, he discovered an infallible prophet of his own, a drunkard named Whitro, who had joined the Prophets by bursting into one of their meetings intending to mock, and then stayed to be converted. Whitro was certainly a rogue who had found in Sir Richard a wealthy old eccentric, and saw an easy way of making him part with his money. He preached a Christianity more literal than any the Church of England has ever cared to embrace, and persuaded the old baronet that the rich could not hope to enter the kingdom of heaven unless they first parted with all their money. Accordingly Sir Richard parted with it; he parted with it to Whitro, who scattered some of it about—for the look of the thing—among the towns and villages that they passed through, and put the rest into his own pocket. Now and again Whitro would perform a miracle to keep Sir Richard's spirits up: on one occasion when their money was temporarily exhausted he produced a gold-piece from the centre of a halfpenny loaf, and the old man was delighted. But Lacy was far from approving of this new prophet or his doctrines. Whitro's inspired command to Sir Richard that he should distribute his estate among the poor was opposed by Lacy, who had received an equally clear injunction from the Spirit that he should do no such thing. The breach grew wider, and Whitro was denounced by the Spirit as a false prophet. One of those who still clung to Lacy had an appalling vision of Whitro "with his Head split in twain, one half hanging over one Shoulder, and the other Part over the other Shoulder." But Whitro, if he ever heard of the vision, probably laughed; he knew all about visions, he had the whole technique at his finger ends. On April 7, 1710, Sir Richard's light, restless, credulous existence came to an end, and with it, one must suppose, the prophetic career of his favourite. The goose, however, had apparently laid most of its golden eggs; for the last we hear of Whitro is that he is riding in his chariot, and has bought a small estate in Buckinghamshire, where the bricklayers are already busy building him a house.

One final shock yet remained to try the faith of those who still clung obstinately to a belief in the Prophets. It had been obvious to all impartial observers from the very beginning that Lacy was strangely attracted by the young prophetess, Betty Gray. She was young and lively, she approved of his agitations and encouraged them; Mrs. Lacy, on the contrary, was now middle-aged and had borne him five or six children, and she had done all she could to induce him to break off his connection with the Prophets. There may have been no more in it than that; but whether the attraction that Lacy felt was of the spirit or the flesh, it was undoubtedly a powerful one. As early as July 20, 1707, he was seen in his agitations to lay his hand upon Betty Gray's head, while uttering a remarkable prophecy:

> Thou art a morning star : thy brightness shall shine throughout this land. I will secure and skreen thy head. When the desolations fall like a cataract about thee, thou shalt not fear. . . . I will pour the oil of my gladness upon thee, when thousands shall be mourning with crys that were never heard before in this place.

Two days later :

> The sun shall not eclipse thy brightness, O thou morning-star. Thou also shalt work miracles in this city. Thou shalt heal the sick. Thou shalt speak languages. Thou shalt speak more elegantly. Thy name shall be chang'd, with a power attending the fact, demonstrating a baptism from on high, even the baptism of the Holy Ghost. Thou must suffer a little while, but I will send an angel, one thou knowest, to clear thee.

And finally, on the following day :

> Everlasting espousals between me and my beloved. I have sought thee, my Love. Oh I rejoice to have found thee, and that thou comest. I will set thee in my throne. I will rejoice over thee from day to day for ever. [*Here Mr. Lacy being under Inspiration, embraces E. Gray.*] The marriage is at hand. King's daughters are among thine honourable attendants. But those that shall be thy companions shall all appear with princely meen, all glorious within, and splendid shining without. . . . I will kiss thee with the kisses of my mouth, my well-beloved. Thy garments shall smell of the fragrancies of odours transcendent. Thou shalt know that thy spouse is Lord of all, because he will bestow it all upon thee. His arms shall embrace thee. Thou art lovely in his eyes, thou fairest of all. The lilly of the vallies, the rose of Sharon, all the rubbies, all precious stones cannot compare with thy lustre. . . . This is a great mystery. Marriage is so when it is declar'd emblematical of the union of Christ with his Church. And as I delight my self over thee, so shall thy panting heart always breath and rise with tenderness, and express itself with transport to discern, to value, to esteem, to delight in my sweet embraces and visits, various various every day. When I speak thy heart shall leap. And when thou speakest I will answer, and when thou callest I will come. . . .

It is little wonder, perhaps, that the Church was shocked at this eighteenth-century Song of Songs, and several critics did not scruple to charge Lacy with bawdiness as well as profanity. Here he was, making his lewd love in public, kissing and fondling this brat from the theatre, using his irreverent mummery to hide the lust in his heart. " When I speak thy heart shall leap. And when thou speakest I will answer, and when thou callest I will come. . . ." What was all this but an indication of his filthy intentions? No, said Lacy, it was the voice of God speaking in parables through the lips of His servant. It must be admitted that Betty Gray's behaviour was hardly such as would strengthen her eligibility for divine favours. To say the least of it, she was highly eccentric. On one occasion she had flung off her clothes and performed the Whore of Babylon before a large gathering of the elect. It appears that she

> took all the chairs in the room, and barricadoed the door, that no body might come in or go out. This done, she laid aside her manteau and night-clothes, tyed up her hair before all the company, with singular modesty; then taking a peruke and hat that she found in the room, put them on her head, and sat down in an elbow chair very majestically, with her arms akembo: After this she rose out of the chair, and for about an hour together thump'd and beat with her fist every one in the room in their turns, except Mr. Lacy; Sir Richard Bulkeley hid himself a while in a corner of the room, in hopes to avoid the effects of her fury, but she finding him out, laid upon him unmercifully, without any regard to his diminutive, infirm corps or his quality, insomuch that he found himself oblig'd to make his escape over the bed, to shelter himself from the hard blows of this termagant Whore of Antichrist.

An odd performance; the romping, one would say, of a hoyden who finds herself unexpectedly applauded for powers that she does not really possess. But Lacy believed in her, and admired her for those eccentricities ; in his eyes she became every day more wonderful, more mysterious. Or had he simply fallen in love with the child ?

Early in 1711 rumours began to get about among the now diminishing Prophets that Lacy had been commanded by the Spirit to do something that would make a great stir in the world. What this was no one quite knew. The word went round that it was a deed of such a kind that " he had rather be burn'd at the stake than submit to it, being such a trial to him and the believers, as never was the like." Was he going to attempt the life of the Queen ? Had he been commanded to set the city on fire ? No ; but it was something equally repugnant to him, something that was trying his faith to the utmost. At last the secret was disclosed. The Spirit had commanded—cruel and almost insupportable burden !—that he should put away his wife, and take to bed Elizabeth Gray, the prophetess, on whom he was to beget children. And so the dim prophecies of 1707 were to be fulfilled after all, and the espousals of Betty Gray were destined to come to pass. They did, in fact, take place some time later. Kings' daughters were not among her honourable attendants, nor did her companions appear with princely mien ; but she was joined to Lacy —" by the Spirit through Mary Keimer "—in some sort of prophetic wedding ceremony. Lacy had already made over the greater part of his estate to his wife and children, retaining only £160 a year for his own uses ; and shortly afterwards he withdrew from London with his new spiritual bride.

This latest command of the Spirit proved, in fact, too much for most of the believers. The women were vexed with Betty Gray, and some of the men were shocked. When finally Thomas Dutton, one of the most respectable of the Prophets, remonstrated with Lacy and then decided to secede, the movement was almost over. Lacy addressed a long letter to Dutton, *A Letter from John Lacy to Thomas Dutton, being Reasons why the former left his Wife, and took E. Gray, a Prophetess, to his Bed;* but the harm was now done. For some time longer he struggled on with his agitations and his prophecies. The Spirit did not fail him in those bad days, but gave him the comforting assurance that the first child begotten by him on Elizabeth Gray should be a son, who should work miracles as soon as he was born. But the luck had turned against Lacy: the promised son proved to be a girl. By this time, however, he had lost all contact with reality, and it is not, therefore, surprising to find the Spirit prophesying to Lacy soon afterwards that the second child would be the eagerly expected son. Again Betty Gray became pregnant, and again the Prophet waited with anxious hope for the birth of that second Messiah. It was not to be: Betty Gray obstinately produced another girl. The Spirit was indeed trying the faith of John Lacy to the uttermost.

Soon the Prophets became only a stale jest, and before long they had dropped out of the news altogether. Many of them, indeed, had gone back to what—after their extraordinary adventures—might almost be called civil life. The original Prophets from France were now scattered, Sir Richard was dead, Whitro kept his chariot, and Lacy had at length retired from the rattle and ridicule of London to live in obscurity with his new wife in the remote parts of Lancashire. Gone were the crowded meetings of the Prophets, the stuffy rooms filled to overflowing with agitated believers, the groaning, the trembling, the sense of a high and dangerous calling, the warm, intimate, exciting consciousness of comradeship. Life was passing on, and the Prophets who had savoured its headiest vintage were now almost forgotten. London still drank and whored and talked politics; the iron rims of coach wheels rattled noisily upon her cobble stones; draymen swore and porters quarrelled; but God had not spoken in fire or thunderbolt, and the streets of the "dear, damn'd distracting Town" ran not with blood, but with the ordinary everyday filth of the kennels. And now the Queen was dead, and a new King, a German from Hanover, was occupying her palace of St. James's. The Tories had fallen, and the Whigs were in power; the coffee-houses buzzed with talk of places and preferment, of trade and stocks and shares. But far away in remote Lancashire Betty Gray continued to breed, and her husband to prophesy. In 1715 he had—or at any rate he published—an obscure vision of the Jacobite troubles; and finally in 1723, he addressed a reply to the Rev. Mr. Owen of Warrington, who had attacked the Prophets. This seems to be his last published work—he died seven years later, in 1730—and it is interesting to find him still, at the age almost of sixty, holding as tenaciously to his claims as ever he did. Some things had not turned out, perhaps, as he and others expected they would; but that did not invalidate the truth of his prophecies. He could explain everything. . . . God's ways are often obscure.

He could explain everything: it is the most remarkable fact about Lacy and others like him that it is quite impossible to convict them of error. If he had not actually faith enough to remove mountains, Lacy had that belief in himself which enabled him to flow round every intellectual obstacle, and continue on his course undismayed. To most of his contemporaries he was simply an impostor; the most enlightened attitude to him may be summed up in the words of one of his critics in the year 1707:

> That which I think comes nearest to Mr. Lacy's case, is a more than ordinary vanity and ambition of being thought wiser and better than the rest of the world, which, join'd with an affectation of singularity, and having the glory of starting something that's odd and out of the way, and being the originals of his own opinion, which he thinks is an infallible proof that the reach of his own understanding is above the common standard, is turn'd at length to subtlety and artifice, to doubling and insincerity, to deceive and being deceived.

There is not much to quarrel with in this verdict; but it is only fair to emphasise the fact that some of those who knew and cordially disliked him were willing to admit the man's sincerity, and one of his bitterest opponents—a man who had wrecked his own career by joining the Prophets, and who now believed that they were completely deluded—was prepared to agree that Lacy was completely innocent even in the matter of Betty Gray, and that when he put away his own wife he did honestly believe that he was obeying the voice of God. It is difficult to account for his uncomfortable and ridiculous career on any other assumption. In a worldly sense he had lost by the year 1711 almost everything; he had given up the society of his wife and children, he had lost his friends and his old station in life, he had signed away the greater part of his estate, and he was committed henceforth to the conversation and society of an ignorant and uneducated girl. He was a jest, a laughing stock,

> A fixèd figure for the time of scorn
> To point his slow unmoving finger at.

Is it too much to suppose that he was supported by that final and invincible consolation, a firm and indestructible belief in himself?

CURRENT INTELLIGENCE

1705-1706

The Ship Worcester, *Thomas Green Commander, is seiz'd in Scotland by the Scots East India Company.*

Yesterday the Colours and Standards taken at Blenheim were carry'd from the Tower to Westminster Hall through a vast Multitude of People.

On Saturday last the Duke of Marlborough, with several of the Nobility, the principal Officers of the Army, and other Persons of Quality, whom his Grace was pleas'd to invite to accompany him, were entertain'd at Goldsmiths Hall with a magnificent Dinner, by the Lord Mayor, Court of Aldermen, and Sheriffs of this City.

Since so many Upstarts do daily publish one thing or other to counterfeit the Original Strop for setting Razors, Penknives, Lances, etc. upon, the first Author of the said Strops doth hereby signifiy . . . .

From New-Market we hear that on Friday Lord Harvey's Spider *won Ld. Granby's* Unicorn. *His Royal H.* Bay Barb *lost to Frampton's Colt. On Saturday Lord Treasurer's* Pouskins *won Parson's* Why Not.

Dr. William Read, Her Majesty's Oculist in Durham-yard in the Strand . . . cures Hair Lips in six days without any Scar, though never so deform'd.

Whereas the Honourable Charles Egerton of Berkley-street in Piccadilly has had the Windows of his House broke several times, but more particularly on the 11*th and* 12*th of this instant, This is to give notice . . . .*

They write from Newmarket that Her Majesty was pleased on Monday last to Honour the University of Cambridge with her

Royal Presence at Dinner. Her Majesty was pleased to confer the Honour of Knighthood on the famous Isaac Newton Esq.

On Wednesday last the Sessions began at the Old-Baily, and ended on Thursday Night, when only one woman received Sentence of Death, for robbing a Gentleman of 4*l., his Watch and Rings, in St. James's Park; since when she has pleaded her Belly. Three persons were burnt in the Cheek, and two whipt.*

There is newly brought over a parcel of choice Canary Birds of divers Colours. . . .

If any Able-Bodied Men are willing to Serve Her Majesty in the Train of Artillery abroad, let them repair to Captain Silver, Master-Gunner of England, at his house in St. James's Park, they shall enter into present Pay of Seven Shillings a Week, and be further Encouraged to Advance as they deserve

Her Majesty's Birthday falling on Ash-Wednesday, the same was celebrated the Day before, being Tuesday last. About Eleven of the Clock a fine Ode was sung, in Consort, before Her Majesty. At Night there was a fine Ball, and a Play acted at Court, and the Evening concluded with Ringing of Bells, Bonefires, and other Demonstrations of publick Joy.

A fam'd Elixir for the Wind, which expels it to admiration, whether in the Stomach or Bowels. All Sour or Windy Belches or Hiccups from Indigestion it removes upon the spot. . . . To be had only at Mr. Spooner's now removed from Black Fryers to the Golden Half-Moon in Buckles-street.

Yesterday was sevennight died John Evelyn Esq.; being about 84 *years of Age. He was an Ornament to this Nation, and to the Common-Wealth of Learning, having made his name famous by the following Composures:* Sylva, *a Discourse of Forrest Trees;* Kalendarium Hortense, *or the* Gardiner's Almanack. . . .

Colonel Richards, Aid de Camp to the Duke of Marlborough, arriv'd here this Afternoon, being sent Express by his Grace from the Camp at Baveshien, with an Account of an entire Victory obtained (by the Blessing of God, on the Arms of Her Majesty and her Allies) on the 12th instant. . . . The greatest Fire was at the Village of Rammelis, of which the Enemy had possessed themselves. My Lord Duke had a great Escape, a Cannon-Ball having taken off Colonel Bringfield's Head as he was remounting his Grace. The Victory was absolute, and the Loss on our side not extraordinary, considering the Sharpness of the Action.

By the Queen, a Proclamation, For a Publick Thanksgiving. Anne R. We do most Devoutly and Thankfully Acknowledge the great Goodness and Mercy of God, who has continued to Us his Protection and Assistance in the Just War in which We are now engaged, for the Common Safety of Our Realms, and for disappointing the Boundless Ambition of France; and hath given to Our Arms, in Conjunction with those of Our Allies, under the Command of John Duke of Marlborough, Captain General of our Land Forces, a signal and glorious Victory in Brabant over the French Army. . . .

Alicant, July 30. On Sunday Morning we took the Town of Alicant by Storm, attacking it by Land and Sea. . . . The Enemy is retir'd into the Castle, and says he'll lose it Inch by Inch; but we have begun to Play with 4 Mortars this Morning, and hope to make him comply shortly.

An Entertainment by Mr. Clinch of Barnet, who imitates the Flute, Double Curtell, the Organ with 3 Voices, the Horn, Huntsman and Pack of Hounds, the Sham Doctor, the Old Woman, the Drunken Man, the Bells: All Instruments are perform'd by his natural Voice. To be seen this present Evening, at 7 a Clock. . . .

Dr. Swift in London

So we all dined together, and sat down at four; and the secretary has invited me to dinner with him to-morrow. . . . They call me nothing but Jonathan. . . . I never knew a ministry do any thing for those whom they make companions of their pleasures.

Journal to Stella

I

On Friday, September 1, 1710, Jonathan Swift stepped ashore from the yacht that had brought him across the Irish Sea, and rode on to Chester. Five days later, accompanied by Patrick, his Irish servant, he was in London. He had ridden on an average thirty-six miles a day. When he set out from Dublin he expected to be home again before Christmas; but almost three years were to pass before he was again taking the road to Chester. And they were to be the most exciting and crowded years of his life.

Swift was already middle-aged; he had passed his fortieth birthday three years ago. Yet, in the eyes of the world, he was a person of no great importance. He had not risen very high in his chosen profession, the Church, and in any gathering of ecclesiastics he was one of those who stood at the back with other parsons of minor rank. It was almost sixteen years now since he had been ordained, and he was still no more than Vicar of Laracor, some six miles out of Dublin, and a prebendary of St. Patrick's Cathedral. Worse than that, he was being forced to spend his life in Ireland. To

Swift, who had grown up in the household of Sir William Temple and had lived from time to time in London, it was something like having a job in the Colonies. He was a sociable man, and Irish society bored him; he was an ambitious man, and he saw little hope of preferment in Ireland. In any case, it was London that really interested him, the London in which his cousin John Dryden had moved, the London for which his old schoolfellow Congreve had written his witty comedies. He had no taste for being a pioneer, a sort of missionary among the Irish natives; he longed for the society of the cultured, of gentlemen who kept good tables and appreciated good conversation.

For though he was rising very slowly in the Church, he was well enough known in the smaller world of literature. To the wits and the booksellers, to a large body of dull and scandalised clergymen and anxious Christians, he was the notorious author of the *Tale of a Tub*. This witty and powerful satire had marked him out once and for all from the common run of amateur and professional scribblers; it had opened a number of doors for him in London, and had firmly and finally closed others. For a young man hoping to make his way in the Church it was a mistake to write the *Tale of a Tub* at all, and a worse one to let it be published; but it is surely too much to expect of an ambitious young author that he should lock up such an astonishing piece in his desk and keep it hidden there indefinitely. Swift enjoyed as much as any man the morning of publication, the pleasure of seeing his work in print and listening to the buzz of commentary. He had, too, a natural delight in shocking the dull and complacent, and an unprecedented talent for doing so. At all events, the *Tale* came out, and it was followed by other almost equally alarming satires such as the *Argument against Abolishing Christianity*. It is true that they were all published without his name on the title-page, but though the jackal may sometimes pass himself off as a lion, it is impossible for the lion to look like a jackal. Swift's inimitable style of thought and expression was soon recognised; and the dull and the pompous upon whom his further preferment depended were more and more scandalised with every fresh outburst of his ridicule. So here at the age of forty-three was Dr. Swift, a writer of enormous power and originality, a man of quite unmistakable intellect, who was yet no more than the vicar of an obscure parish in Ireland, and, in the opinion of many devout Churchmen, lucky even to be that.

But now at last he was being given his chance to rise in the Church. The Archbishop of Dublin had sent him to London on a mission of great importance for the Church in Ireland. In 1704 Queen Anne had granted a remission of the Crown's right to the First Fruits in England, and they were being used to augment small benefices; it was in the hope that he might be able to negotiate a similar concession for the Irish clergy that Archbishop King was now employing Swift. It was not the first time he had tried. On his previous visit to London two years before, he had been commissioned to approach the Whig Ministers with the same request, but he had found them disinclined to give the Irish Church something for nothing. This time, perhaps, he would be more successful.

Swift lost no time in setting about his business, but he could hardly have arrived at a less opportune moment. The Whig Ministry of the Earl of Godolphin was already tottering. Godolphin himself had just been dismissed, and the remaining Ministers were too much concerned about their own desperate state to spare much time for the petition of an Irish parson. " Everything is turning upside down," he wrote on September 9, " every Whig in great office will, to a man, be infallibly put out ; and we shall have such a winter as hath not been in England." Godolphin in particular was in no mood to trouble himself with Church affairs. It was owing to his impeachment of the high Tory clergyman, Dr. Sacheverell, that he had lost office, and the remission of the Irish First Fruits may well have seemed to him just about the last thing he wanted to recommend : the Church had had more than its share of triumph for the time being. Besides, it was the Irish Church that Swift had come to him about, and the principle that Irish affairs can always wait was already a commonplace with English statesmen. With some of the other Whig Ministers Swift was on better terms, and the more discerning among them were anxious to retain his services for the party. Hitherto Swift had been a Whig, and such political writing as he had undertaken was all in the Whig interest. There had been some talk of rewarding him with an Irish bishopric, but nothing had come of it ; and rightly or wrongly he felt that the Whig Ministers were rather ashamed of their past treatment of him. At present, however, they could obviously do little for him, and Swift settled down to await developments.

Meanwhile he began looking up his old friends in London. On the Sunday after his arrival he sat with Addison and Steele until after ten, and the following day he dined at Addison's lodgings. Swift, who never paid for his dinner if he could help it, ate frequently with Addison during the next few weeks, and in spite of the fact that he was apparently less of a Whig these days than Addison would have liked, they remained for some time on the old friendly terms. Steele was more difficult. He was a much more violent party man than the moderate Addison, and these were trying days for the Whigs. At no time had Swift been more than loosely attached to the Whig interest; and now, as he began to realise that if anything was to be done about his First Fruits it would have to be done by the Tories, he must have felt less comfortable in the presence of a party man like Steele. For some time he continued to have his letters addressed to Steele's office, and they still met occasionally, but the friendship was becoming strained. "We shall have a strange winter here," he prophesied, "between the struggles of a cunning provoked discarded party, and the triumphs of one in power; of both which I shall be an indifferent spectator, and return very peaceably to Ireland, when I have done my part in the affair I am entrusted with, whether it succeeds or no." The first part of his prophecy was true enough, but the rest was ludicrously wide of the mark. Before many weeks had passed Swift was to be anything but an indifferent spectator.

One by one the Whig Ministers were turned out of office, and the smaller fry, like Steele (who held the post of Gazetteer) had their jobs taken from them, and were replaced by Tories. Soon there was talk of a general election. Swift saw that there was nothing for it but to wait; he could only do harm to his case by bringing it forward in the middle of a political crisis. "Things are in such a combustion here," he wrote on September 22, "that I am advised not to meddle yet in the affair I am upon." So he dined still with his friends, and walked the streets, and prowled round the bookshops, and amused himself in his lodgings at night by writing a lampoon on Godolphin or a *Tatler* for Steele. There was no particular hurry; the Archbishop's business could wait.

II

What separates us from the past more than anything else is the fact that we almost always see it as we see a landscape from the top of a hill. We habitually look at the past from a distance; we can rarely feel that we are standing in the very middle of it, being jostled by the passers-by, splashed by cart wheels, drenched by the rain or warmed by the sun. What the past needs is more triviality and less importance. When, as sometimes happens, the trivialities have been preserved for us, it is generally in the diary of some conscientious nobody; it is rare, indeed, to have a day-to-day record of the life of any great man.

But that is just what we do have with Swift. For almost three years we know pretty nearly everything that happened to him, from the time that he got out of bed in his London lodgings and said his prayers until the time that he fell asleep again at night. We know all this because of a correspondence that was never meant for our eyes at all, and that reveals in surprising detail the thoughts and feelings of the most remarkable Englishman [1] of his generation. We have only one side of this correspondence, but it is Swift's. His letters—or "journals"—were addressed to two maiden ladies in Dublin, Esther Johnson and Rebecca Dingley.

Esther Johnson was at this time twenty-nine years old. She had gone over to Ireland with her friend Dingley in 1701, and the two women were now living together in Dublin. "Stella," as Swift was to call her, was the daughter of Sir William Temple's steward, and when

[1] Though born in Dublin, Swift preferred to think of himself as English.

her father died she was brought up in the Temple household. When Swift first went to Moor Park in 1689 to act as Temple's secretary, Stella was a child of eight. She was fourteen years younger than Swift, and the relationship between the two seems to have been fixed by those earliest years at Moor Park. Swift is the daring adult; it pleases him to go on thinking of Stella as the delightful and rather naughty child. Perhaps it was Swift's way with the women he loved; but in the whole of his correspondence with Stella one feels that he is addressing a mere child, and not a young woman of independent means and marriageable age. He had taken charge of her education at Moor Park, and he remained the kindly master addressing his favourite pupil.

Dingley, a lady of mature years, comes in for a certain amount of good-humoured banter in the course of the correspondence; she was clearly something of a joke—to Swift, to Stella, and, after the manner of comfortable middle-aged ladies enjoying good health but not very clever, to herself. It was not perhaps a very gay or fashionable establishment that the two ladies kept; but they had their little circle of friends in Dublin, and the days passed pleasantly enough. There were jaunts to the country in the summer, and card parties, and there were dinners at Dean Stearne's, or Archdeacon Walls', or Alderman Stoyte's. But for Stella, at any rate, the happiest moments of her life were spent with her old friend of the Moor Park days, that friend who teased and scolded her, who looked after her money for her, who advised and directed her in every matter of importance. Swift was a constant visitor, and the two of them (with Dingley as a sort of benevolent presence in the background) shared a whole world of fun and little intimacies.

The Dublin folk were expecting him to marry her. As the years passed and they still lived apart, the word went round among the malicious that Stella was Swift's mistress, and among the more charitable that she had been secretly married to him.[1] The idea that the two could have remained all those years merely good friends seemed incredible to the eighteenth century, and still puzzles, or disappoints, the twentieth. Few men have had their actions criticised more unsparingly than Swift; everything that he did or failed to do has seemed to some of his critics to take on a sinister significance. Yet if his relations with Stella were not necessarily so abnormal as most of his biographers have made out, they were at least peculiar. And if he did not want to marry her himself, he certainly did not want anyone to take her from him. What her loss would have meant to him can best be realised by reading the so-called *Journal to Stella,* with its intimacies, its store of common experience, its affection and tenderness, its family jokes, and its "little language." Few letter-writers have come so near to bridging the gulf of distance as Swift did in those letters written over a period of almost three years to a woman he certainly loved, whether or not she was ever his wife or his mistress.

III

But Swift had not come over to England just to write affectionate letters to Stella. He had his work to do; he had to dance attendance on Queen Anne's Ministers until he interested one or more of them sufficiently to speak to the Queen about the First Fruits. As things now were in England, the man who was most likely to

[1] 1716 is the date usually given.

get the affair put through for him was Robert Harley, and Harley was a Tory. Forced to resign from the Godolphin Ministry two and a half years ago, he had just come back to office as Chancellor of the Exchequer on the fall of Godolphin. He was the man of the moment; and when Swift learnt on September 30 that Harley was willing to see him he must have realised that politically he was at a parting of the ways. He was not going to make things difficult by standing firm on Whig principles. He had got little enough out of the Whigs—and the Tories knew it. "I am already represented to Harley," he told Stella, "as a discontented person that was used ill for not being Whig enough; and I hope for good usage from him. The Tories dryly tell me I may make my fortune, if I please; but I do not understand them, or rather, I do understand them." Swift was willing enough to make his fortune; but at the moment he was thinking more of his commission from the Irish bishops. The interests of the Church were above party differences, and if the Tories were the likeliest men to secure the First Fruits for the Irish clergy, he must apply himself to the Tories. Swift, of course, was no child politically; he realised that Harley would probably expect some *quid pro quo*, that he would try, in fact, to detach him from the Whig party. Well, what if he did? Swift had always been a Whig with certain reservations, and the links that attached him to the party were more in the nature of personal friendships than political principles.

Harley was not long in dealing with the First Fruits to Swift's satisfaction. By the last week of October he had assured him that the Queen would grant the concessions that the Irish bishops were asking for, and on November 4 Swift wrote to Archbishop King to say that the matter was now settled. Actually, it was far from having been finally disposed of; but some months later the formalities were at last completed, and Swift's mission had ended in entire success. Now, surely, he was free to return to Laracor, and the ladies would be seeing him again every day, and hearing from his own lips about all the people he had met in London. But Stella knew better. As early as November 30 he had hinted to her that he had become "a little involved" in political affairs.

> O Lord! does Patrick write of my not coming till *spring?* Insolent man! he know my secrets? . . . Faith, I will come as soon as it is any way proper for me to come; but, to say the truth, I am at present a little involved with the present ministry in some certain things (which I tell you as a secret), and soon as ever I can clear my hands, I will stay no longer. . . . But, to say the truth, the present ministry have a difficult task, and want me etc. Perhaps they may be just as grateful to others: but, according to the best judgment I have, they are pursuing the true interest of the publick; and therefore I am glad to contribute what is in my power. For God's sake, not a word of this to any alive.

On January 16 he writes again to say that he is at home, God help him, "every night from six till bedtime, and has as little enjoyment or pleasure in life at present as any body in the world, although in full favour with all the ministry." Clearly, Stella realised, he must be writing something. He was, indeed. On November 2 Swift had taken over the *Examiner*, the leading ministerial journal, and he continued to write every number until June of the following year.

The *Examiner*, which appeared weekly, had been founded three months before to advocate the cause to which the Ministry was most deeply committed—peace with France. Week after week Swift was stating with devastating force the case against prolonging the war, and he must have gone a long way towards preparing the public mind for the peace which was ultimately signed in the Spring of 1713. The line that Swift intended to take was made perfectly clear in the very first number that he wrote. The war, he reminded his readers, was dragging on from one campaign to another. Why? The answer could only be, Because it paid certain people to keep it going. Who, in fact, stood to lose if peace were declared to-morrow? The military men; not the rank and file, of course, but the officers. Swift was soon to press his charges home more particularly against the Duke of Marlborough, who had already, he reckoned, got away with over half a million pounds of the nation's money, and whose appetite for glory was equalled only by his thirst for wealth. Swift was not, of course, so rash as to deny that Marlborough was a great soldier; but behind the romantic general leading his devoted troops from victory to victory he showed the greedy adventurer ruthlessly building up his own private fortune. Marlborough, however, was only the chief villain of Swift's Tory drama. Behind him were huddled the Whig financiers, the men who were lending the nation money at interest, and behind them again the noisy crew of stock-jobbers and Change Alley men. "Let any man," Swift writes,

> observe the equipages in this town, he shall find the greatest number of those who make a figure to be a species of men quite different from any that were ever known before the revolution; consisting either of generals and colonels, or of those whose whole fortunes lie in funds and stocks; so that *power*, which according to the old maxim was used to follow *land*, is now gone over to money. . . . So that if the war continue some years longer, a landed man will be little better than a farmer of a rack-rent to the army and to the public funds.

It was this new moneyed interest more than anything else that Swift was fighting; he saw the change that was coming over English society, and he resisted it with all his might. In doing so he was serving the cause of Harley and the Tories, but he was also expressing his own honest convictions. Harley was "pursuing the true interest of the public."

But Swift, it will be objected, had not merely ceased to be a lukewarm Whig; he had rapidly developed into a warm Tory. In return for the good offices of Harley with the Queen he was now turning out whole-hearted propaganda for the Tory party. Had he, then, been bribed? The truth on this occasion is not so crude as all that. In the autumn of 1710 Swift suddenly found himself in a position that he would probably have reached by gradual stages even if he had never met Harley and been swept into the stream of contemporary politics. For a man holding Swift's views on Church and State the Tory party was the natural home. It is quite obvious that he had come to an understanding with Harley; but what Harley wanted of him was what Swift was honestly prepared to give—what he was, in fact, delighted to be asked for—his intelligent co-operation in a political programme of which he entirely approved. Swift hated war, he had the intellectual's distaste for soldiers, unless (as very rarely happened—with the Earl of Peterborough, for instance) they were also men of wit. He yielded, therefore, only too easily to the Tory outcry against the greatest soldier of his age. Caught up in the whirl of party intrigue, no doubt he overstated the case against Marlborough and the war-mongering Whigs, but all that he said had at least a firm basis in personal conviction. "Few of this generation," he reminded Stella, "can remember anything but war and taxes, and they think it is as it should be." England had been winning glorious, but, on occasion, very bloody victories; there were bonfires in the streets, and the bells were ringing in all the churches, but was England any happier for it, or more prosperous, or more Christian?

Such consideration weighed powerfully with the man who, fifteen years later, was to put into the mouth of the King of Brobdingnag his terrible comments on Gulliver's countrymen. With all its faults, the Tory party was honestly attempting to put an end to a futile and costly war. But what counted even more with Swift in his conversion to the Tory party was the personal factor. From the very beginning Harley had treated him with a charming friendliness. The cold, punctilious Godolphin had repelled him; the genial and apparently off-hand Harley surprised and delighted him. When he came to know the more brilliant and astonishing St. John, he was perhaps still more impressed. The friendship of those great men—the two chief ministers of State—and the knowledge that he was being consulted by them on matters of the highest importance, released emotions in him which had long been starved. As a youth he had grown up in the household of Sir William Temple; and though Temple, the retired statesman and the great Whig gentleman, had many virtues, and must have taught him a good deal, he was too far apart in age and rank and temperament from his secretary to be on very easy terms with him. The ageing Temple must often have vexed a young man, already conscious of his own great powers, with his air of authority and his too settled opinions. He was, in fact, a more humane and philosophical Godolphin, a man who kept one in one's place, and insisted—though ever so politely—on his own importance. "Don't you remember," Swift wrote to Stella, "how I used to be in pain when Sir William Temple would look cold and out of humour for three or four days, and I used to suspect a hundred reasons? I have pluckt up my spirit since then, faith; he spoiled a fine gentleman."

Since Temple's death, it is true, Swift had occasionally moved in the most important Whig circles. He had come to know such men as Halifax, Somers, Sunderland, and Wharton; but though he might occasionally dine at their tables, he was still separated from them by the gulf that divides a minister of State from a country parson. It was perhaps the chief delight of his new friendship with Harley and St. John that almost at once he was on terms of easy familiarity with them, and saw them in their most unguarded moments. They called him "Jonathan," and laughed at his jokes. When they chaffed him he would pay them back in their own coin, for he had always a way of saying whatever came into his head. They told him once that they had been speaking to the Queen about him, and had found that she had never heard of him: that, Swift told them, was their fault, not the Queen's. Their ease and affability impressed him enormously. Looking back at his old patron of the Moor Park days, so prim and dignified, he could not help contrasting him unfavourably with those two cheerful, almost amateur, statesmen, and thinking what a "splutter" Temple used to make about being a Secretary of State. Sometimes, indeed, their apparent lightheartedness alarmed him. "I cannot but think they have mighty difficulties upon them," he confided to Stella, "yet I always find them as easy and disengaged as schoolboys on a holiday." Whatever their limitations, Harley and St. John had the stuff of which great politicians are made: they had the imperturbability of the public man, the power to conceal their anxiety in a crisis, and, in large measure, the sanguine temperament which prevents that anxiety from ever arising. Swift, with his sudden bursts of optimism and gaiety alternating with fits of gloom and misgiving, was a man born to worry. He admired the level, carefree temperament of Harley because it was so utterly unlike his own. Temple may have spoilt a fine gentleman, but no amount of training would have turned his secretary into a European statesman. He was at his best behind the scenes, where, in fact, he was now. His advice, when Harley sought it, might modify policy; but his real value lay in his remarkable power to advocate with his pen the agreed policy of the Tory ministers, and to cast contempt on that of the opposition.

He was indeed busy during those first few months in London; for the *Examiner* was only the most important of his writings for the Ministry, and what he had no time to write himself he handed over to Tory hack-writers like Mrs. Manley. And in spite of all his headaches and colds in the head and occasional fits of giddiness, he was having a wonderful time. He had suddenly become a person of the highest importance. Noble ladies sought an introduction to him, and kept inviting him to dinner; people that he had never seen before claimed acquaintance with him, or bowed to him in the coffee-houses; place-hunters, knowing that he had the ear of the ministers, were continually soliciting him to further their applications. He intervened successfully on behalf of many of his old Whig friends who were in danger of losing their employment. His correspondence was increasing every day; he rarely returned to his lodgings now without finding several letters waiting for him. When a rumour went the rounds that he was going to preach before the Queen, there was a crowded Court. Even the Whig newspapers were beginning to take notice of him personally. It was all very exhilarating, and Swift was revelling in this new and animated life, and hoping that it would last. Now and again, it is true, there came a characteristic reaction from this world of politics and intrigue, a sudden slump in his confidence, a sense of futility. "I am half weary of them all," he told the two ladies in Ireland at the beginning of his second winter in London. "I often burst out into these thoughts, and will certainly steal away as soon as I decently can." But only a few days later he is telling them frankly that if *they* were not in Ireland he would not think of the place twice a year.

IV

As the weeks and months pass, and the Irish Sea still separates Swift from Stella, one might expect the tone of his letters to grow less intimate. But Swift carries on the one-sided conversation on paper with unabated liveliness. As he sits up in bed, scratching away on the paper with his quill pen, Stella and Rebecca Dingley are constantly before his eyes. When he is writing to them, he says, he is always happy. "It is just as if methinks you were here and I prating to you, and telling you where I have been." And again: "I can hardly imagine you absent when I am reading your letter, or writing to you. No, faith, you are just here upon this little paper, and therefore I see and talk with you every evening constantly, and sometimes in the morning, but not always in the morning, because that is not so modest to young ladies."

For three years Swift was living in two worlds: the world of Harley and the *Examiner*, of the Queen and the Court, of coffee-houses and footmen and landladies; and that other world which came stealing back to him at the end of the day, as the fish glide back to their old haunts under the willows when the last noisy boatload of trippers has gone splashing past for the day—the quiet world of Stella and Dingley, of his fishponds at Laracor and the quickthorn hedges that he had planted. "Pshaw, pshaw," he writes almost exactly eight months after his arrival in London, "Patrick brought me four letters to-day: from Dilly at Bath; Joe; Parsivol; and what was the fourth, who can tell? You old man with a stick, can you tell who the fourth is from? Iss an please your honour, it is from one madam MD,[1] Number Fourteen." On a certain cold January morning he wakens before daylight, fumbles in the dark for his candle, lights it, and proceeds to "prate" to his two ladies. Sir Andrew Fountain is sick; Atterbury, they say, will be made Dean of Christchurch in Oxford, though the College would rather have Smalridge; Prior made a good pun t'other day to Lord Carteret. . . . And then:

> I think I am bewitched to write so much in a morning to you, little MD. Let me go, will you? and I'll come again to-night in a fine clean sheet of paper; but I can nor will stay no longer now; no, I won't, for all your wheedling: no, no, look off, don't smile at me, and say, Pray, pray, Presto,[2] write a little more. Ah! you're a wheedling slut, you be so. Nay, but prithee turn about, and let me go, do: 'tis a good girl, and do. O faith, my morning candle is just out. . . . God Almighty

[1] In the *Journal* "MD" stands for Stella and Dingley.

[2] "Presto" in the *Journal* stands for Swift. It is said to have been the name given to him by the Duchess of Shrewsbury, an Italian lady, who was unable on one occasion to recollect the English word for "Swift," and used the Italian equivalent.

> bless you etc. What I am doing I can't see ; but I'll fold it up, and not look on it again.

The *Journal* is full of such intimacies. When Swift is in high spirits (as he frequently is during those busy years in London) Stella and Dingley might almost be in the next room. At any rate he gets a great deal of pleasure from pretending that they are, and that he is really talking to his " dear little brats " :

> So I'll rise, and bid you good morrow, my ladies both, good morrow. Come stand away, let me rise : Patrick, take away the candle. Is there a good fire ?—So—up a-dazy.

Again and again in the *Journal* there are streaks of gaiety, moments of delightful humour and extravagant folly. He was as fond of jesting about Queen Anne as later generations have been. " There was a drawing-room to-day at Court," he writes to the ladies,

> but so few company, that the queen sent for us into her bed-chamber, where we made our bows, and stood about twenty of us round the room, while she looked at us round with her fan in her mouth, and once a minute said about three words to some that were nearest her, and then she was told dinner was ready, and went out.

It is a memorable picture, memorable for its deliberate flatness : the semicircle of gentlemen making their bows, the middle-aged widow with her fan in her mouth, turning her head slowly like an automaton. Swift was never presented to the Queen, but he delighted in making irreverent allusions to his familiarity with her. " The Queen made me a curtsy," he tells the scandalised ladies in Dublin,

> and said, in a sort of familiar way to Presto, How does MD ? I considered she was a Queen, and so excused her.

Or again, some months later, when he was staying at Windsor :

> The Queen and I were going to take the air this afternoon, but not together, and were both hindered by a sudden rain. Her coaches and chaises all went back, and the guards too : and I scoured into the market place for shelter.

Or he returns to his favourite fooling when a letter arrives from Stella :

> Coming down the Mall, who should come towards me but Patrick, and gives me five letters out of his pocket. I read the superscription of the first, Pshoh, said I ; of the second, Pshoh again ; of the third, Pshah, Pshah, Pshah ; of the fourth, A Gad, A Gad, A Gad, I'm in a rage ; of the fifth and last, O hoooa ; aye marry this is something, this is our MD. . . .

One is reminded of Keats or of Lewis Carroll writing to their sisters ; the tone is that of the serious but affectionate adult amusing himself by amusing a little girl.

The greater part of the *Journal* appears to have been written from his bed—after he had slipped into it at night, or before he had got out of it in the morning ; and no doubt this habit helped him to maintain the intimate and informal tone. But he seems to have done some of his more serious writing in bed, too. Like many another man who has been hard up in his youth, Swift remained for the rest of his life extremely frugal in his habits. To say that he was " careful " is to understate the position ; he was often parsimonious. To see his coals blazing up the chimney filled him with misgivings for the future. These Londoners thought nothing of keeping a fire burning all day in an empty room ; but to Swift a coal fire in his sitting-room was something of an event, and the hour at which it must be lit a question to be considered carefully in advance. " I have gotten half a bushel of coals," he tells the ladies, " and Patrick, the extravagant whelp, had a fire ready for me ; but I pickt off the coals before I went to bed." Stella must have been teasing him about his habit of saving coal, for some weeks later he writes in a spirit of comic bravado : " Come, come, young women, I keep a good fire ; it costs me twelve-pence a week, and I fear something more ; vex me, and I'll have one in my bed-chamber too." On such occasions Swift is making fun of his own frugality, and consciously exaggerating it ; but he is jesting in self-defence. It was the same story the following winter. By the middle of October he was telling Stella that the weather had turned very cold, but that he was determined not to have a fire in his room until November. He seems to have held out successfully ; and when at last he was compelled to order a fire, he got some loose bricks and stuck them at the back of the grate " for good husbandry."

What he could save he did. A good deal of this great man's energy was consumed in avoiding what Dr. Johnson once described as " the fatal waste of fortune by small expenses, by the profusion of sums too little singly to alarm our caution." The day was a failure on which he had to pay for his own dinner. In the course of three years, passed almost continuously in London, he can hardly have spent more than ten pounds on his food.[1] He was, of course, in great demand, as one of the wittiest talkers in London, and, later on, as one who had the ear of the ministers ; but Swift never made any bones about looking for a dinner, and if he found that his companions left him to pay his share at an eating-house he was indignant—or so, at least, he indicated in his

[1] Setting aside such extraordinary occasions as the day on which he entertained the Brothers' Club. After almost a month in Town, Swift was able to tell Stella (on October 2), "It has cost me but three shillings in meat and drink since I came here."

letters to Stella. Up to a point he was justified. He was mixing for the most part with men much richer than himself, and such men were apt to forget that if they could order a bottle of wine at five shillings and pay for it without a second thought, the Irish parson whose company they found so entertaining was a comparatively poor man who could not afford many such expenses. "There's a young fellow here in town we are all fond of," he wrote to the ladies,

> and about a year or two come from the university, one Harrison, a little pretty fellow, with a great deal of wit, good sense, and good nature ; has written some mighty pretty things. . . . The fine fellows are always inviting him to the tavern, and make him pay his club. Henley is a great crony of his : they are often at the tavern at six or seven shillings reckoning, and always makes the poor lad pay his full share. A colonel and a lord were at him and me the same way to-night : I absolutely refused, and made Harrison lag behind, and persuaded him not to go to them. I tell you this, because I find all rich fellows have that humour of using all people without any consideration of their fortunes ; but I'll see them rot before they shall serve me so.

As a parson, Swift was in a special position. The man of God was not, perhaps, entitled to a free dinner wherever he went, but most gentlemen probably felt that among laymen he should hardly be expected to pay his reckoning. At any rate, what with dining by invitation with the Queen's ministers, and throwing himself upon the hospitality of his friends and acquaintances, Swift managed to cost himself very little in food and drink while he was in London.

It was less easy to save money on coach-hire. Hackney coachmen and chairmen made no allowance for his cloth, and Swift was continually grumbling about the cost of merely getting about the Town. "Lord Halifax," he complained, "is always teazing me to go down to his country house, which will cost me a guinea to his servants, and twelve shillings coach hire; and he shall be hanged first." Whenever he could, he walked, not only to save money, but because he loved the exercise; but in wet weather he was often forced to hire a coach. "'Tis plaguy twelve-penny weather this last week," he writes, "and has cost me ten shillings in coach and chair hire." And again: "This rain ruins me in coach hire; I walkt away sixpennyworth, and came within a shilling length, and then took a coach, and got a lift back for nothing."

But if Swift was constantly alarmed at this dribbling away of his money in small expenses, he had the utmost sensitiveness about being indebted to any man. He might expect his friends to give him a dinner, but God help them if they tried to give him money. The well-meaning Robert Harley blundered badly, just three months after he had met Swift, by sending him a bank bill for fifty pounds. No doubt Swift's complaints about the expensiveness of everything in London—wine, wigs, tips for footmen, coal, lodgings, coach hire, food—were not made to Stella alone. No doubt, too, Harley was accustomed by this time to seeing Swift arrive for an appointment drenched to the skin, or with his boots spattered with mud. We happen to know the condition in which he first waited upon Harley, for with his usual complete honesty in those matters he told Stella the whole story. As Harley had agreed to see him at four o'clock, he could not accept any invitation to dinner for that day; but it never occurred to him to celebrate the event by dining well for once by himself. In fact, he carried a ballad that he had just written to Benjamin Tooke, his printer, hoping that Tooke might ask him to stay to dinner and allow him to leave early ; but Tooke was not at home. "I was forced," he writes to Stella, "to go to a blind chop-house, and dine for ten-pence upon gill-ale, bad broth, and three chops of mutton ; and then go reeking from thence to the first minister of State." No wonder if Harley, accustomed to the scented elegance of the Court, thought that an occasional note for fifty pounds might relieve his new friend of such disturbing economies. A Defoe would have made no bones about accepting such a gift ; but in Swift Harley had to deal with a highly sensitive and complex character. Whatever he might write in later years about the insufferable pride of man, Swift had his own share of it ; and in money matters he had to be handled with the utmost tact. On this occasion, at any rate, the bank bill was indignantly returned. "Mr. Harley desired I would dine with him again to-day," he told Stella,

> but I refused him, for I fell out with him yesterday, and I will not see him again till he makes me amends. . . . I was this morning early with Mr. Lewis of the secretary's office, and saw a letter Mr. Harley had sent him, desiring to be reconciled ; but I was deaf to all intreaties, and have desired Lewis to go to him, and let him know I expect further satisfaction. If we let these great ministers pretend too much, there will be no governing them.

It was not that he did not expect some reward for the service he was rendering ; but that reward must be such as a gentleman would feel himself entitled to accept, and not the sort of charitable gift that is made to a poor relation. It is characteristic of Swift that on the very day that Swift told Stella of his quarrel with Harley he should also have told her that he had been forced to spend two shillings on coach and chair hire, and even then had walked till he was dirty.

The fascination of the *Journal to Stella* often lies in such contrasts. Swift returns from Court, where he has been joking with noble ladies and ministers of State, to his humble lodging and the drunken and execrable Patrick; he suddenly turns aside from some important question of national policy to worry about some trifle that a Harley or a St. John would have dismissed from his mind without a second thought. He has all the small yet persistent worries of the bachelor. He is "heartily vexed" over the minor mishaps of life: the parcel that goes astray, the "puppy" whose letter has to be answered, the carelessness of servants. For several months in the *Journal* there are frequent references to a "box" that had got lost between London and Chester. He had bought a number of things for the ladies—chocolate, a bottle of palsy-water, spectacles for Stella, tobacco for Dingley. He had packed them up in a box, and entrusted them to a friend who was returning to Ireland; the friend was to hand it over to another friend who was going on to Dublin. But somehow or other the box miscarried, and Swift's natural irritability with the incompetent was increased by frequent reminders from Stella and Dingley that the palsy-water and the tobacco had not yet come to hand. "The Devil burst Hawkshaw," he breaks out on New Year's Day, 1711. "He told me he had not the box,

> and the next day Sterne told me he had sent it a fortnight ago; Patrick could not find him t'other day, but he shall to-morrow. Dear life and heart, do you teaze me? does Stella teaze Presto? That palsy-water was in the box; it was too big for a pacquet, and I was afraid of it breaking. . . . I'll never rest till you have it, or till it is in a way for you to have it. Poor dear rogue, naughty to think it teases me; How could I ever forgive myself for neglecting any thing that related to your health? Sure I were a Devil if I did—— See how far I am forced to stand

> from Stella, because I am afraid she thinks poor Presto has not been careful about her little things: I am sure I bought them immediately according to order, and packt them up with my own hands, and sent them to Sterne, and was six times with him about sending them away. . . . Indeed, Stella, when I read your letter, I was not uneasy at all; but when I came to answer the particulars, and found that you had not received your box, it grated me to the heart, because I thought through your little words, that you imagined I had not taken the care I ought.

Three months later the box is still missing. In October Sterne is passing through Chester: Swift begs him to inquire about the box. A week or two later, another and more reliable friend on the way to Ireland is given the same commission. "I hate that Sterne for his carelessness about it," he tells the ladies, "but it was my fault." On November 7 he is brooding about it still. "A murrain take that box; every thing is spoiled that is in it." The mystery of the box is never cleared up. No doubt it was lying somewhere between London and Chester, waiting for someone who never came to claim it, until finally some inquisitive soul broke open the lid and examined the queer consignment, and there was the bottle of palsy-water and the spectacles and the mouldering chocolate—none of them, as the eighteenth-century advertisers for lost bank bills were fond of putting it, of any value save to the owner. But to Swift the loss of the box was one of those small tragedies that leave a permanent scar; it was of the stuff of which an old man's memories are made, as he lies dying and delirious on his bed. . . . The box! Stella's box! The Devil burst Hawkshaw!

The box was only one of Swift's worries. A perpetual source of exasperation was Patrick, the Irish servant that he had brought with him from Dublin. Patrick (it is just as well) lived before the days of modern journalism; otherwise some clever reporter would certainly have hunted him out in later years and got from him the exclusive story of his life with Dr. Swift. What Patrick would have had to say about his master is not hard to guess. He would certainly have complained about his unaccountable outbursts of irritability, his meanness, his way of finding fault with a poor fellow that always tried to serve him faithfully; there would have been an account of how Dr. Swift often sat up late into the night writing, and perhaps some gossip about the lady that lived a few doors away, a Mrs. Vanhomrigh and her daughter. What we do know, however, and with considerable detail, is what Swift thought about Patrick. The earlier references to him are genial enough, though from his first arrival in London Patrick seems to have drunk more than was good for him. It is clear that he had a good friend in Stella, for Swift several times warns her that if Patrick goes on as he is doing it will be no use trying to intercede for him any more. He oversleeps in the morning, he is out at night when Swift wants him to carry a message, he is terribly extravagant with coals, he is continually drunk. But it is clear that he was not just a nit-wit, for Swift reports on one occasion that Patrick was reading Congreve's plays. And he had his endearing qualities. He had bought a linnet for Dingley, and intended to carry it back to Dublin with him.

> It was very tame at first, and 'tis now the wildest I ever saw. He keeps it in a closet, where it makes a terrible litter; but I say nothing: I am as tame as a clout.

It is unlikely that Dingley ever got her linnet, for, after repeated warnings, Swift was at last compelled to turn his man off. The crisis came one night in October, 1711, when Swift, who had been out all day, returned to find that the door of his lodging was locked, and that the absent-minded Patrick had gone off with the key.

> I cooled my heels in the cloisters till nine, then went in to the musick-meeting, where I had been often desired to go ; but was weary in half an hour of their fine stuff, and stole out so privately that every body saw me ; and cooled my heels in the cloisters again till after ten : then came in Patrick. I went up, shut the chamber door, and gave him two or three swinging cuffs on the ear, and I have strained the thumb of my left hand with pulling him, which I did not feel until he was gone. He was plaguily afraid and humbled.

Patrick weathered that storm, as he had weathered many a smaller one ; but in April of the following year he was finally dismissed. No doubt he was an idle fellow ; but he had at least given Swift something to grumble at without fear of contradiction. It was one of the functions of the eighteenth-century servant. In justice to Patrick, it should be admitted that he had chosen to serve an exacting master. What Swift habitually thought of his own and other people's servants appears in his bitterly ironical *Directions to Servants*, written many years later. The longest chapter deals with the misdeeds of footmen ; and the shade of poor Patrick, with his drooping Irish lip and his flushed drunken face, flits constantly before the eye :

> When you are in lodgings, and no shoe-boy to be got, clean your master's shoes with the bottom of the curtains, a clean napkin, or your landlady's apron.

> Never ask leave to go abroad, for then it will be always known that you are absent, and you will be thought an idle rambling fellow ; whereas, if you go out and nobody observes, you have a chance of coming home without being missed. . . .

> When you are ordered to stir up the fire, clean away the ashes from betwixt the bars with the fire-brush.

> If you are sent to the post-office with a letter in a cold rainy night, step to the alehouse and take a pot, until it is supposed you have done your errand ; but take the next opportunity to put the letter in carefully, as becomes an honest servant.

For a proper understanding of Swift's mind, his comments on eighteenth-century servants are highly significant. He was a man who hated muddling and incompetence and idleness and dirt and waste ; and he associated all of these with servants in general, and perhaps with Irish servants in particular.

There were many occasions during his long stay in London when he was horribly uncomfortable in his lodgings. " Patrick tells me my caps are wearing out," he complains to Stella, " I know not how to get others. I want a necessary woman strangely ; I am as helpless as an elephant." Four days later—it is in the depth of November—he draws an even more depressing picture of his circumstances :

> Last Saturday night I came home, and the drab had just washed my room, and my bed-chamber was all wet, and I was forced to go to bed in my own defence, and no fire : I was sick on Sunday, and now have got a swinging cold. I scolded like a dog at Patrick, although he was out with me : I detest washing of rooms : can't they wash them in a morning, and make a fire, and leave open the windows ? I slept not a wink last night for hawking and spitting : and now every body has colds. Here's a clutter. . . .

And there are other gloomy occasions when his chimney smokes, or his wine has turned sour, or he arrives home soaked to the skin. No wonder that he sometimes curses the ministers, and longs to be back in Dublin or Laracor, where Stella and Dingley would see to it that he was properly looked after.

V

But there was one family in London that softened the rigours of Swift's bachelor life very considerably. On his previous visit to London he had made the acquaintance of Mrs. Vanhomrigh, the widow of a Dublin merchant; and now on his return he settled down in a lodging only a few doors away from her. On September 25 he remarks casually to Stella, "I was so lazy to-day that I dined at next door." It was the first of many dinners "at next door," and the beginning of an intimacy that was to end in misery and frustration thirteen years later. The danger to Swift's peace of mind came, not from Mrs. Vanhomrigh, who seems to have been a friendly, hospitable soul, but from her eldest daughter. In 1710 Esther Vanhomrigh—the second Esther in Swift's life—was not much past her twenty-first birthday. But to be twenty-one is to be a woman, not a child; and this woman was soon to spoil what Swift almost certainly meant to be no more than a playful friendship by inconsiderately falling in love with him. It must be admitted that he gave her every opportunity. He was always dropping into dinner on one excuse or another: it was too wet to go anywhere else, or it was too hot to walk into the City, or he wanted to avoid some puppy who had invited him to eat at a tavern. "Out of mere listlessness," he told Stella, "I dine there very often." In the Strand one night he fell over a tub and broke his shin. "I will dine with Mrs. Vanhomrigh till I am well," he wrote to Stella, adding what she must have known well enough by now, that Mrs. Vanhomrigh lived "but five doors off." When in the summer of 1711 he took lodgings in Chelsea, he still kept his best gown and periwig at her house, and there was no break in their acquaintance.

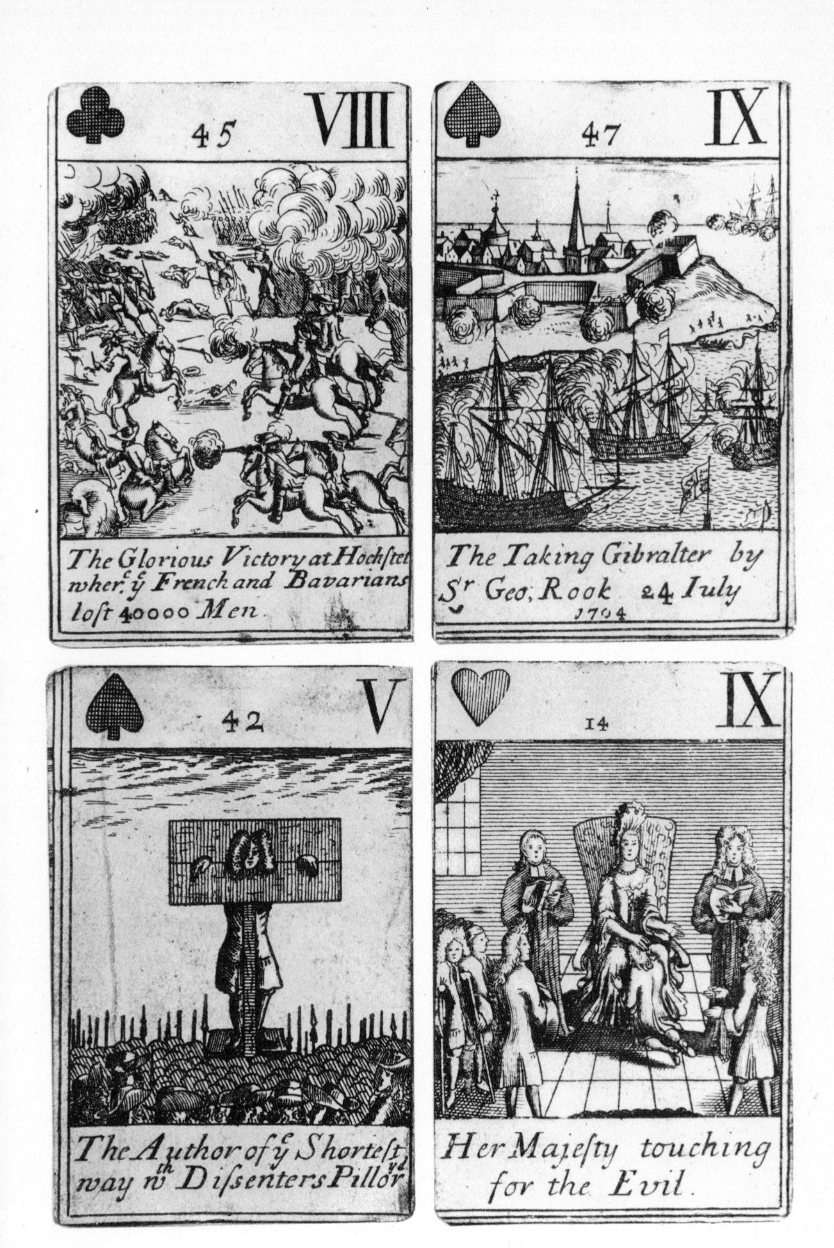

QUEEN ANNE PLAYING-CARDS (2)

It was this man, so grave and yet so full of fun, so charged with public affairs and yet so delightfully unconventional at her mother's table, that Esther Vanhomrigh was seeing almost every day. To Esther—he now called her " Vanessa "—Swift's visits were rapidly becoming the one thing that mattered in the day's business. To Swift—so far, at any rate—Vanessa was merely an intelligent girl, whose mind he was helping to form, as he had helped to form Stella's. He enjoyed her company, he was flattered, no doubt, by her admiration and her dependence on him, he watched with satisfaction her intellectual development, and the way in which she caught and reproduced the very idiom of his thought. But did he ever pause to consider that this young woman might be falling in love with him ? Did it never occur to him that Mrs. Vanhomrigh might, with some justification, be hoping that one day her daughter might marry this brilliant parson who seemed so clearly marked down for high preferment ? When a man has no thought of marriage himself he is often surprisingly blind to the fact that everyone else is expecting him to marry some particular woman. Swift, too, was more than twenty years older than Vanessa ; it was natural enough that he should still think of her as a child. And he was a parson, a privileged person where women are concerned, whose frequent presence in a household of women need not of necessity lead to expectations of marriage. Yet Swift, it will be said, was a singularly clear-sighted man ; he could hardly have been ignorant of the impression that he was making in the Vanhomrigh household. One can hardly believe that he remained unaware for long of Vanessa's rapidly growing affection ; but a penetrating insight into the human mind is not incompatible, particularly among men, with a surprising insensibility in personal relationships.

What, for instance, is one to make of this? On February 2, 1711, he describes to Stella, with all his strange detachment, an incident that seems highly significant now, but to which he seems hardly to have given a second thought. "When I got home," he writes,

> Mrs. Vanhomrigh sent me word her eldest daughter was taken suddenly very ill, and desired I would come and see her; I went, and found it was a silly trick of Mrs. Armstrong, lady Lucy's sister, who, with Moll Stanhope, was visiting there: however, I rattled the daughter.

This was on February 2, not April 1; and if one reconstructs the background of this incident, it is not difficult to see what was in the mind of the too playful Mrs. Armstrong, aided and abetted by Moll Stanhope and the other ladies. Yet Swift himself apparently thought of it as nothing more than a "bite"; or so he would have Stella believe. And so surely he did believe, or else why mention it to Stella at all?

Swift's relationship to Stella will probably always remain a mystery; but Stella is perhaps a sufficient reason for his never marrying Esther Vanhomrigh. Swift could be entirely ruthless with other people's feelings; but however much he may have hurt Stella by his actions, one gets the impression that she was the one person above all whom he always tried to spare from unhappiness. Married to him or not, she was an effective barrier between him and any other woman, and all the more effective because she was so dependent upon him. Swift's biographers have accused him of many faults, but none has so far suggested that his emotions were superficial; if he loved, or if he hated, he did so with the whole force of a powerful and tenacious character. By the year 1710 Stella had become part of his life; she could not be displaced. But Stella was in Dublin, and

Swift in London. There were plenty of intelligent young women in London, and Swift enjoyed being in their company and " rattling " them. No doubt his freakish humour was not to every woman's taste, and there were some, in fact, who loathed him. But there were others—the Lady Betty Butlers, the Moll Stanhopes, the Vanhomrighs—to whom this whimsical parson was the best company in the world. The truth is, Swift seems to have succeeded in keeping the two worlds of London and Dublin apart in his mind, just as he was afterwards to keep Stella and Vanessa from ever becoming acquainted with each other. For the present, at any rate, he seems to have been willing enough to enjoy Vanessa's company with no thought of any possible complications in the future. Vanessa was a diversion, a kitten that one picks up and plays with at the end of the day's work. It was pleasant to banter her, to make fun of the books she was reading, to sit with her after dinner and teach her some philosophy or some history, but she did not occupy his thoughts during the day : one does not think of absent kittens. The other and larger world that began outside the Vanhomrigh's front-door kept Swift in a state of continual excitement. And those closing years of Queen Anne's reign were not lacking in incident.

VI

On the afternoon of March 8, 1711, Robert Harley was sitting on a committee of the Council, examining a half-mad Frenchman, the Marquis de Guiscard, who had been accused of carrying on a treasonable correspondence with the French Court. All at once, before anyone had time to stop him, Guiscard leant over and stabbed him near the heart with a penknife. Fortunately for Harley he was wearing a thick embroidered waistcoat, but the wound was serious enough. For several days he lay in some danger of his life, and Swift was in an agony of grief and anxiety. As for Guiscard, several of the lords had promptly run him through the body with their swords; and though he was afterwards patched up by a surgeon, he died in Newgate about a week later. Cheated of a spectacular trial, the Ministry nevertheless managed to make some political capital out of the attack on the Lord Treasurer: Guiscard's dead body became for several days one of the raree-shows of London. "We have let Guiscard be buried at last," Swift wrote to Stella, "after shewing him pickled in a trough this fortnight for two pence apiece; and the fellow who shewed would point to his body, and, 'See, gentlemen, this is the wound that was given him by his grace the Duke of Ormond; and this is the wound etc.' and then the show was over, and another set of rabble came in." Clearly Swift was not the only man with a genius for publicity in those eventful days.

On the whole, Harley's accident was a piece of good luck for him; it undoubtedly increased his popularity, and silenced for some months the criticisms of his discontented supporters. Yet in the long run it probably weakened his position; for while he was slowly recovering his strength St. John was more active than ever, and consolidated his personal influence over the more extreme elements in the Tory party. These angry gentlemen, disgusted with Harley's policy of moderation, and anxious to see the huge Tory majority in the House used more to the disadvantage of the Whigs, had formed themselves into a noisy and insistent caucus, called the October Club. They met frequently, drank October beer, made speeches to each other, sang songs, and called for a more vigorous Tory policy. Harley might laugh at them, but they certainly worried Swift. "The Ministry is upon a very narrow bottom," he told Stella, "and stand like an isthmus between the Whigs on the one side, and violent Tories on the other. They are able seamen, but the tempest is too great, the ship too rotten, and the crew all against them." As the weeks passed and those Tory followers of Harley's who wanted to lead him became more and more of a nuisance, Swift (who had secretly a good deal of sympathy with some of their demands) was apparently instructed to head them off. This, at any rate, is what he did, with a great deal of skill, in a twopenny pamphlet, *Some Advice Humbly Offer'd to the Members of the October Club*. The clamour died down.

The climax of his political career came in the winter of 1711-12. Harley, back at work again, was pushing ahead with his negotiations to bring a long, glorious, and costly war to an end. The Whigs, whether they wished it or not, were committed to being the "war party," and were bitterly resisting every step that the Ministry took towards peace. The nation at large, fed for years on Marlborough's glorious victories and on Whig propaganda against the French, was still prepared (if reluctantly) to let the war go on till the French were beaten to their knees. If the Ministry was to gain any credit in the country for giving it peace, its first concern must be to make the war much more unpopular than it actually was. This was the task now entrusted to Swift; and in a masterly pamphlet, *The Conduct of the Allies*, he carried it out with magnificent success.[1] Published on November 27, 1711, it had sold eleven thousand

[1] This pamphlet is, of course, only an extension of the work he had been doing in the *Examiner*.

copies within three months. Swift did not pitch his arguments too high for the average man ; he appealed, in fact, to what was most practical and unheroic in his fellow-countrymen, to what must always appeal to the average man—and perhaps with particular force to the average Englishman—his pocket. The nation, he reminded his readers, was almost ruined. Our troops won battle after battle, and yet our situation was growing more and more desperate ; we were on the point of expiring with all sorts of good symptoms. We kept on taking towns for the Dutch instead of being content to carry on the war at sea, our natural province as a maritime nation. We had poured out English lives and English money in a war which was going to benefit the Dutch and our other allies far more than ourselves.

> It will, no doubt, be a mighty comfort to our grandchildren, when they see a few rags hung up in Westminster-hall, which cost an hundred millions, whereof they are paying the arrears, to boast as beggars do, that their grandfathers were rich and great.

Tell an Englishman that he is acting selfishly, and he will probably shrug his shoulders. But tell him that he is behaving in an absurdly quixotic fashion, that he is ruining himself and endangering the safety of his country to save—or, still worse, to enrich—a pack of foreigners, and you will almost certainly make him thoroughly ashamed of himself. And if you add that he is simply being imposed upon by those foreigners, that they are merely taking advantage of his innocence or his good-nature, you will have convinced him that he has been acting with the greatest folly. Swift drives home his points with merciless simplicity. On the one side, victories, prestige, bonfires ; on the other, poverty, taxation, profiteers, mutilated bodies, the Dutch and the Emperor growing fat and prosperous, and poor old England paying the piper. Much of this was true, and most of it Swift believed; but he was not above exaggerating in a good cause. The ways by which a nation is extricated from a war are sometimes no less unscrupulous than the ways by which they are pushed into one.

Peace came at last in the spring of 1713, and Swift's—and Harley's—work was done. It was two and a half years now since he had arrived in London, intending to stay for a few weeks only; and all this time he had been working for the Ministry. Now it was time to look for his reward. If promises counted for anything his future was assured, but he was still no more than Vicar of Laracor. As early as May, 1711, he had told Stella frankly that "to return without some mark of distinction would look extremely little; and I would likewise gladly be somewhat richer than I am." Some months later he was writing enviously of his friend Atterbury in his "warm quiet deanery." What Swift was hoping for, the rest of the world was beginning to expect. His own Archbishop in Dublin saw fit to waive any responsibility he might have for Swift's preferment in the Church by the simple expedient of advising him to help himself. He should take the first opportunity of pressing his claims to Harley; but if he really wanted to rise in the Church he should also make a point of writing a book on some new subject in Divinity. "You will find," he wrote,

> that it will answer some objections against you, if you thus show the world that you have patience and comprehension of thought, to go through with such a subject of weight and learning.

8

The inference was only too obvious: the works that Swift had published so far (not forgetting the *Tale of a Tub*) were hardly stepping-stones to high advancement in the Church. In such terms might the professor suggest to his young assistant that in academic circles a study of Milton's prosody would be of more service to him than the clever detective story he had just written. Swift, who had long since taken the measure of Archbishop King, was exasperated with this officious prelate. "A rare spark this, with a pox!" he wrote to Stella. "But I shall answer him as rarely." This matter of his preferment was becoming a sore subject with Swift.

By 1712 he had become less diffident about urging his claims. In February he got so far as to ask Harley for the deanery of Wells, which, along with those of Ely and Lichfield, was then vacant. According to eighteenth-century standards he had more than earned his deanery; but Harley, as usual, procrastinated. To add to his annoyance, word actually got about that he had been appointed to Wells, and he was put to the trouble of replying to premature congratulations. They were indeed premature. Month after month passed, and still the three deaneries remained unfilled. At last, however, in April, 1713, the leisurely Harley settled the matter with the Queen. On the morning of April 13, his secretary, Erasmus Lewis, called on Swift, and—as one friend to another—showed him the warrants for the three deaneries: Swift's name was not on the list. At noon he met Harley in the secretary's office, and Harley said "many things too long to repeat." But Swift had heard them all before. He told Harley firmly that unless the long-promised preferment was granted him immediately he would pack up and return to Ireland. Harley must have realised that he had tried Swift's patience as far as it would go, for when they met again an hour later at the Duke of Ormond's dinner table he told him that the three warrants had been stopped, and that he intended to push through Swift's appointment that evening. He could not have one of the English deaneries because the Queen would not allow it; but the present Dean of St. Patrick's in Dublin would be made Bishop of Dromore, and Swift would succeed him at St. Patrick's. Dublin was a poor exchange for Wells, but Swift had come to see that it must now be that or nothing.

Now began what must have been very nearly the most trying ten days that he had ever spent. He had been driven at last by disappointments and delays to a frame of mind in which the deanery of St. Patrick's, which he had once despised, seemed a valuable prize. But would he get it after all? Harley's positive assurances had failed him so often in the past that they might fail him again now. The two Archbishops were his enemies, and no doubt they had impressed upon the Queen that Dr. Swift's preferment would not be for the good of the Church. Harley, of course, was his friend, but how much of a friend? How hard was he trying?

The best clue to what was happening—or what Swift thought was happening—is to be found in the agitated scraps of news that he jotted down for Stella. "I write short journals now," he admits, "I have eggs on the spit." On the 14th Harley had promised that his appointment would be settled that night. ("So he will for a hundred nights. So he said yesterday, but I value it not.") The following day Swift learnt that what was holding things up was the question of whether he should be Dean of St. Partick's, or (as Harley would have preferred) a Canon of Windsor. ("I told him I would not stay for their disputes.") On the 16th the Queen told the Duke of Ormond, who had the deanery in his gift, that she was willing that Swift should be Dean of St. Patrick's; and then Harley saw fit to hold everything up again by begging that he should be Prebend of Windsor. On the 19th the Duke of Ormond, who had hitherto been quite willing that Swift should be dean, suddenly developed scruples about the present Dean of St. Patrick's, whom he did not like, becoming a bishop—even to make room for Swift, whom he did like. On the 22nd, however, the Queen ordered that the warrant to make him Dean of St. Patrick's should be drawn up. This was good news, but Swift kept his head. ("While it is delayed I am not sure of the Queen, my enemies being busy.") This time, fortunately, there was no hitch. On the following day Swift heard that all the warrants had been signed, and that the Duke of Ormond's order to make him dean was on its way to Ireland. So it was done at last. "I was at Court to-day," he was able to tell Stella on the 26th, "and a thousand people gave me joy, so I ran out." For the next few days he was, as he puts it, thoroughly "bedean'd."

VII

His friends might be wishing him joy, but Swift's own emotions seems hardly to have risen above relief. For the last few months there had been less and less fun in his letters to Stella. There were snatches of the old gaiety, of course, but the note was rather one of weariness, or anxiety, or even disgust. No doubt the novelty of his situation had worn off; the condescension of the great men no longer seemed so surprising, the intimate dinners with the Lord Treasurer had become part of a regular routine. But there were other reasons for his increasing gravity. A painful attack of shingles had lowered his vitality in the spring of 1712, and he was being frequently troubled by attacks of giddiness. Undoubtedly he had been overworking. Party feeling, too, was becoming more bitter, and Swift found himself dragged into a painful quarrel with Steele in the summer of 1713, which resulted in both men attacking each other in print without mercy.

What was worrying Swift more than anything else, however, was the growing coolness between the two chief ministers. It is a long story, of confidence withheld on the one side, of petty jealousy and unsatisfied ambition on the other; but from being a loyal subordinate St. John (now Viscount Bolingbroke) had come to be a rival, and he was looking forward with growing impatience to the time when the slow, scheming, compromising, procrastinating, crab-like Harley would give way, and leave others to carry out a more active policy. Temperamentally the two men were very different, and the wonder is that they worked together so well, and so long, as they did. Swift had been uneasily aware for many months that the friendship between the two ministers was not so cordial as it might appear from their smiling appearance in public. As early as August, 1711, he was exerting himself to prevent an open quarrel between the two men. Their misunderstandings and jealousies, however, continued to give him anxiety, and by the summer of 1713 it was common knowledge that the two chief ministers were at loggerheads.

It was in those gloomy circumstances that Swift, in the month of June, returned to Ireland, and was installed Dean of St. Patrick's. Of his meeting again with Stella, and of what passed between them during the rest of that summer, nothing is known. But apparently Swift had returned to Dublin in wretched health, and less inclined than ever to put up with the various "puppies" who harassed him with their impertinent congratulations and their idle conversation. He retired to his willows at Laracor, apparently determined to forget London and everyone in it. To what extent Vanessa contributed to his gloom it is impossible to say; but her letters followed him to Ireland, and as the days passed and she got no reply they became more importunate. She was a woman, passionate and possessive; she loved him, and had no intention of concealing the fact. Stella, no doubt, was better trained; she had accepted Swift's idiom of affectionate banter, and had accommodated her own feelings to it. But this younger pupil was not to be so easily restrained. If Swift felt nothing more than affection for Vanessa, her letters in the summer of 1713 must have made him terribly uneasy; if, on the contrary, he loved her as she wanted to be loved, the problem of Stella's future must have distressed him profoundly.

Nor was he allowed to forget the heart-breaking muddle that Harley and St. John were making of their affairs. Letters kept arriving from Erasmus Lewis begging him to return at once, and so prevent a complete split in the Ministry. Swift was most reluctant to make a move. He kept putting off his departure, until Lewis was almost in despair. At length, however, he roused himself to action. Early in September he was back in London again.

He found that Lewis had not exaggerated the seriousness of the situation. Harley and St. John had drifted into a state of passive hostility; and Harley's immense talent for political manœuvring was now being employed as much against his rival as against the Whigs.

The Whigs, too, were taking heart. As the winter came on the Queen became seriously ill, and the question of the succession became the one engrossing topic of conversation. The Whigs, who had always taken a firm line in support of the Hanoverians, were now accusing the Ministry of having plans ready to bring in the Pretender. Before long Swift found himself compelled to answer a violent pamphlet of Steele's, and he delivered a last devastating attack on his old friend in *The Public Spirit of the Whigs.*

From now on he watched with growing distress the steadily widening breach between the two chief ministers. "A ship's crew quarrelling in a storm," he wrote, "or while their enemies are within gunshot, is but a faint idea of this fatal infatuation." Fond though he was of Harley, he saw now with increasing clearness how much his secretive, backstairs diplomacy—"this reserved, mysterious way of acting, upon points where there appeared not the least occasion for it, and towards persons, who, at least in the right of their posts, expected a more open treatment"—was responsible for the misunderstandings that had arisen in the Ministry. But such tactics had become second nature to Harley; he must do things in his own indirect way or not at all. Swift found it hard, too, to forgive Harley for frittering away the power of the Tory party. Finding himself at the head of a large and enthusiastic majority of Tories, he had almost gone out of his way to exasperate them by his tenderness for the Whigs. A moderate policy was all very well, and in 1710 it was probably necessary; but now that the Whigs were gathering strength the only course was to unite the whole body of the Tories by taking a strong party line.

But Harley's hour had passed. He was still the same

old schemer; but he was gradually losing his grip, and many of his old friends were giving him up in despair. He had always been a hearty drinker, and now he was drinking too much. The Queen, in fact, had begun to complain that he often came drunk into her presence, and failed to treat her with proper respect. Swift knew all this, or most of it; but he could not forget Harley's many kindnesses to him, his friendliness, the wonderful times they had spent together concocting mischief, or laughing at each other's jests. "In your public capacity," he wrote to Harley just before the crash came, "you have often angered me to the heart, but, as a private man, never once."

For St. John he had apparently less affection, but he had a real respect for his ability. The man was something of a rake; yet for all his apparent idleness he did not let his pleasure interfere with business. He was extraordinarily well read, a magnificent speaker, and a great worker when the occasion arose. Given time, he would probably weld the Tory party into a great force, as Harley never could or would. For all his love of Harley, Swift was no doubt hoping that the struggle between the two men would end in the triumph of St. John. But it was a hideous thing to watch. Swift did what he could, went from one to the other, remonstrated, warned, begged, threatened; but the situation steadily deteriorated.

At last he could bear it no longer. On June 1 he suddenly left London, and went to stay with an old friend, the Rector of Letcombe Bassett in Berkshire. Harley had been given over by his physician: Swift had realised that the case was now hopeless, and had retired from the scene to wait for the inevitable outcome of events. His friends in London kept him well posted with news; they, too, were now watching hopelessly the last struggles of Harley as he grappled with his younger and more active rival. The odds against him were now heavy. St. John had won over Lady Masham to his side, and Lady Masham had now more influence than anyone else with Queen Anne. On July 27, after a long and painful altercation in the presence of the unhappy Queen, Harley was forced to give up his office, and St. John—still a young man of thirty-six—was left in control of the political field.

Never, perhaps, in all her life had the Queen been so important as she was at this moment. And the important thing about her was that she was still alive, still Queen of England, a sure and effective barrier against the Whigs and against the Hanoverian family, whose coming would wreck the hopes of St. John and his Tory followers. St. John, it is true, had not the confidence of all the Tory party by any means; but he was a man of great gifts, an experienced administrator, young, ambitious, and full of energy. If his luck had held he would probably have changed the course of English history. But the incalculable happened. The crisis had proved too much for the Queen; and scarcely had the defeated Harley withdrawn from her presence than she was seized with a dangerous illness. For the past two years rumours about her health had been sending the bank stock up and down with alarming rapidity. This time there was to be no recovery. Worn out with anxiety, child-bearing, and a complication of diseases, Queen Anne could struggle on no longer. On the morning of Sunday, August 1, 1714, the news ran through the Court that she was dead.

VIII

With the death of the Queen Swift and his friends went into political exile; and though he was to live another thirty years he was never again to see the Tory party in power. Looking back now, at a distance of more than two hundred years, one may see no more reason to admire the Tories of Queen Anne's reign than the Whigs. But if Swift himself remained critical of the men who were putting a Tory policy into practice, he did genuinely believe in what the Tories stood for—or in what, at any rate, he was persuaded they did stand for. His sense of despair at the eclipse of the Tory party was not merely the gloom of the politician whose side had been "in" and was now "out." In the overwhelming return of the Whigs to power he saw the triumph of all those forces of darkness against which he had always fought: the money-lenders and the stock-jobbers, a selfish morality, a cynical religion, hypocrisy and corruption. The shadow of Robert Walpole was already falling across the path of English history.

His friends scattered, his political usefulness destroyed, Swift withdrew to his deanery and to Stella. But even the old happy relationship with Stella was not to continue unchallenged; it was threatened now by the passionate Vanessa, who was soon to follow him to Ireland, and pursue him with protestations and entreaties. The clouds were indeed gathering over his head; the sun was never again to shine on him with quite the old brightness. The golden days of 1710-13 would never return.

Everyone who has felt the attraction of Swift has felt also the need of finding some clue to explain his strange, intense, and uncompromising character. There is no "key" to Swift; but one can account—at least in part—for that gloom and bitterness which coloured so much of his writing. Ruthlessly honest, he could find no refuge in an easy optimism, or a pious hope that "all was for the best." Had he cared less about mankind, he might have taken a cynical pleasure in exposing the short-comings of the human race; but he cared deeply, and he suffered in proportion. For a man like Swift the chances of happiness are always precarious: the danger is always that his mind will be driven to brood perilously on those thoughts that his own relentless intelligence compels him to face. The first two years that Swift spent in London working for Harley were almost certainly the happiest in his whole life. He was happy because his hands were full, because his thoughts were turned to immediate and practical ends, and he was living in a world of action. Thought was not then a disease; his powerful mind was being exercised in the open air of political strife, and it was all the healthier for that exercise. *The Conduct of the Allies* is magnificent; one cannot imagine anything more effective of its kind. But only "of its kind." What the world has remembered of Swift is not *The Conduct of the Allies* but *Gulliver's Travels;* and *Gulliver's Travels* comes from that other Swift who wrote, not for Harley and the Tories, but for himself and mankind, who gazed with shame and horror on human depravity and refused to be comforted. The price of *Gulliver's Travels* was Swift's unhappiness, his spiritual despair; it came from a mind brooding in solitude. Had Swift continued to bustle about actively in a world of Whigs and Tories, of politics and intrigue, there might have been no Gulliver at all. "Faith," he might well have exclaimed as he turned over the pages of the *Voyage to the Houyhnhnms*, "Robert Harley nearly spoilt a great satire."

CURRENT INTELLIGENCE

1707–1708

Yesterday the Queen came to the House of Peers, whither the Commons being sent for, Her Majesty gave her Royal Assent to the Act for an UNION *between the two Kingdoms of Scotland and England.*

Letters from Portsmouth advise that the Association *was unhappily lost near the Rock of Scilly, with Sir Cloudesly Shovel and her whole Crew.*

The Country Fellows belonging to the Islands of Scilly, finding Sir Cloudesly Shovel's Corps, took a fine Emerald Ring from off his Finger, and buried him Seven Foot deep in the Sand; but quarrelling about the said Ring. . . .

On Monday next, being the first Monday in January, will begin to be Preach'd at St. Paul's Cathedral, the Lecture founded by the Honourable Robert Boyle Esquire deceas'd, for the Year 1708.

For the Benefit of Mr. Pinkeman, By Her Majesty's Royal Company of Comedians, At the Theatre-Royal in Drury-Lane, this present Thursday, being the 8th *of April, will be presented a Comedy, call'd,* The Stratagem . . . *With a new Epilogue, spoken upon an Ass by Mr. Pinkeman. And by her Majesty's Command, no Persons are to be admitted behind the Scenes.*

Tunbridge-Wells, July 6. *An Account of the Glorious Victory*[1] *gain'd by the Duke of Marlborough over the French*

[1] The Battle of Oudenarde.

in Flanders arriving here this Day, the Nobility and Gentry order'd a Bonfire to be erected on the Top of the Hill, in which was 7 Waggon Load of Wood, and in the Evening they all repair'd to the Place, and drank the Queen's, the Prince's, and the General's Healths, 5 great Guns firing at every Health. Several Barrels of strong Beer were distributed among the People, who express'd their Joy by louder Acclamations and Huzza's than had been ever observ'd before at this place.

This Day, about twenty Minutes after one of the Clock, the Prince of Denmark departed this Life. His Royal Highness had been troubled for many Years with a constant difficulty of Breathing, and sometimes with Spitting of Blood, which often endangered his Life. About three Months since a dropsical Humour. . . .

The most Noble Volatile Smelling-Bottle in the World, which smelled to, Momentarily fetches the most dismal Faintings, or Swooning Fits, and in a Minute removes Flushings, Vapours, Dullness, Head-Achs, Megrims etc. . . . in a Word, the greatest Cephalick, Stomatick, Hepatick, and powerful Aromatick possible. Is only sold at Mr. King's, at the Globe Picture Shop in the Poultry near Stocks-Market over-against the Church.

In Pursuance of an Order of the Right Honourable the Lords of Her Majesty's Most Honourable Privy-Council, appointed to consider of the Interment of his Royal Highness Prince George of Denmark, This is to give Publick Notice, That it is expected that all Persons . . . do Cover their Coaches and Chariots, and Chairs, and Cloath their Livery-Servants, with Black Cloth, by Sunday the 14th of this Month: And that no Person do use any Varnish'd or Bullion Nails to be seen on their Coaches, Chariots or their Chairs. . . .

The Last Years of Joseph Addison

. . . nor youth nor age,
But, as it were, an after-dinner's sleep,
Dreaming on both.

Measure for Measure

If Addison is a writer in no immediate danger of being forgotten, he is one that is not very actively remembered. He manages, indeed, to keep his place, but that place tends more and more to be the schoolroom, where his writings serve the purposes of higher education by supplying examples of seemly and elegant prose. Addison liked to do good, but he can scarcely have envisaged this sort of usefulness for his graceful and epicene essays. Yet there they remain, stuck fast in the literary consciousness of the race, like some household heirloom not quite precious enough to arouse enthusiasm, and yet too well-made just to be thrown away. We needn't look, and usually we don't; but Addison's essays are always there to be glanced at if we happen to be in the proper frame of mind.

We may, of course, blame ourselves for this indifference to a writer whom our grandparents held in high esteem. We are accustomed, no doubt, to grosser pleasures, more violent stimulants than Addison's pellucid prose can afford; we have no time to watch the mellow eighteenth-century sunbeams playing ever so delicately across his blameless page. All this, and much more, may be true; and Addison's ghost rises with gentle admonishment to remind us of our moral and cultural shortcomings. But if he awakens no more than a faint response to-day, the fault is partly his own. Time has faded his colours as it has not faded those of Swift or Defoe. Nor did he ever work very much in the primary colours; his effects were almost all gained with the faint and hesitating tints that are proper to the more intellectual of the emotions. One must not be indelicate in writing about Addison, but the man lacked guts. He stood for the little intimacies and the unobtrusive graces; love and anger seem to have been alike outside his range. In an age of splendid hatred and contempt—an age that produced as two of its characteristic works *Gulliver's Travels* and *The Dunciad*—Addison steered a decent middle course, refraining, wherever possible, from any frank exposure of his feelings. But unless Pope and others were mistaken, there was also that in Addison which prompted him to pursue behind the scenes petty enmities which he never allowed to come into the open; he was ready to

> Damn with faint praise, assent with civil leer,
> And without sneering, teach the rest to sneer;
> Willing to wound, and yet afraid to strike,
> Just hint a fault, and hesitate dislike;
> Alike reserv'd to blame, or to commend,
> A tim'rous foe, and a suspicious friend.

Pope has often been blamed for allowing those terrible lines to stand so long after Addison was dead, but there were few in his own day who were prepared to deny that the accusation was substantially just. Addison was what the world generally calls a good man, but he was never a spontaneous one; on the other hand, even with Pope's lines to help one, it is not easy to persuade oneself that he was a bad man. If he occasionally wounded in the dark, he also, like Ralph Allen, did good by stealth ; he was the sort of man to whom distressed people turned with some hope of success. Among the letters that Addison preserved—or, more accurately perhaps, that he failed to destroy—there is one from an old landlady of his who had fallen upon evil days. She had been left a widow with three small daughters, whom, as she reminded him, he had seen " tho' not perhaps to remember them " ; but what with taxes, and repairs, and tenants running away without paying their rent, she was now almost destitute. Casting her thoughts about, she continues, she could not fix them on a more generous and public spirit than his own good self ; and so she makes her plea to him—

> which I hope will raither move your pitty than incur your displeasur—as it will give you a farther opertunety to distinguish your self from the common Rank of mankind which in the whol cours of your life has hetherto been so obvious and so much admir'd, among which number is none of the least tho the meanest of—
>
> Sr.
> your devoted most obedient
> humblest Servants,
> Grace Bartlett.

What Addison did about it we have no means of knowing ; but one tends, perhaps, to preserve the letters one has not answered, and knows one ought to answer, rather than those whose business one has dispatched. If Addison had settled Mrs. Bartlett's troubles for her, we should probably never have had the chance of reading her letter. He was certainly generous enough on other occasions, handing his share of the profits from *Cato* to the players, and giving a purse of guineas to Milton's daughter ; but normally he quite failed to be so spectacular, and took his noiseless path to Westminster Abbey among murmurs of general admiration and approval, but with only an occasional cheer. And yet—among Whigs, at any rate—he was well liked. So popular was he, indeed, in the year 1710, that Swift could write to Stella: "Mr. Addison's election has passed easy and undisputed; and I believe, if he had a mind to be chosen king, he would hardly be refused."

But in 1710 Addison was only thirty-eight, and at thirty-eight a man should be fit for most things, even, if necessary, to be Prince Consort to Queen Anne. It is the last few years of his life that really give him away, hinting at weaknesses in his character that might otherwise have remained unsuspected by all but his closest friends. If he had died while putting the final touches to a *Spectator* essay, it might have been much more difficult to say just what it was that Addison lacked. Up to the year 1716 his life had been an almost unqualified success. He had been doing admirably what he was best fitted to do, writing, talking, transacting a little public business, and doing it all quietly and elegantly, without fuss or hurry. His essays in the *Tatler* and the *Spectator* were among the foremost ornaments of polite literature; his dignified tragedy of *Cato* had in 1713 a quite remarkable reception from the Town. At Button's Coffee-House he presided over a circle of secondary wits, the "little senate" of Pope's famous lines. Addison, in fact, had got on. He had not pushed himself forward ostentatiously; it was rather that he always managed to be in such a position that he was inevitably pushed from behind. When the news of Marlborough's famous victory at Blenheim reached London, the Ministry looked about for a poet to give it suitable publicity. Lord Halifax told Godolphin that there was only one man for the job, and Addison, then in his thirties, was commissioned to celebrate the victory. The result was his poem, *The Campaign*, which brought him both fame and preferment. It was the same with his celebrated essays. Steele had started the *Tatler* on his own, and when he found the task of supplying the printer with material three times a week growing irksome he naturally looked to his friends for help. And so Addison got his chance to prove that he was an essayist. Things kept happening to him in this way ; he waited quietly in the background, and when the occasion arose he stepped forward to take a hand. He did what was asked of him ; and if he surprised at all, it was by doing the thing better than anybody had imagined it could be done. Even *Cato* was more or less dragged out of him. He had written the first four acts many years before while he was still at Oxford, and it was only in response to the pressure of his friends that he at last consented to complete the play with a fifth act.

Had he only kept on in this way, sailing before a gentle wind and leaving the initiative to his friends, he might have remained a successful and contented man. He had his own little circle in London, his favourite haunts, his dinners and suppers and visits to the playhouse. And in the summer there was Bilton. He had bought this pleasant little estate in Warwickshire for £10,000, and he was laying it out with taste and discrimination. Letters would arrive from his steward full of respectful suggestions about hedging, ditching, draining, thatching, ploughing, tiling, planting, sowing, and fencing. The wind has blown down a great tree, but it was much decayed ; the fields would be all the better of " a sprinkle of dung " ; three brace of partridges have just been sent off to him by Horton the carrier. There is that troublesome business of Perkin's cottage, and "the house where Ramsdon did live," which is ready to drop unless something is done; and there is the important matter of the fish ponds and the pigeons.

"Iff my Responces com too thick upon," you his steward writes to him from Bilton,

> Please to Snub me, for the Writeing is not my talent, I never know when to leve off, but this is in answer to your last as to your ffish-ponds. I am Sorry to tell you, they are lower now than they were at Midsumer, for the great pond is Sunk more than 5 foot in depth, and the other 2 proportionately Empty, and yet there heads are very good and does not Leake a ffirkin in a day; but still there is a Sufficient quantaty of Water for the ffish, for non of em die. Most of the Wells are drie, and in many places they want Water for there Cattell, wee are Expecting Raine every day for tis very much wanted, but when it coms your ponds will be full very quickley; before I had youres I had putt some Roach into the pond you mention'd, and as Soon as I can get any pike I'le put them into the same place and I'll not faile fix Stakes, Rootes, etc. in the bottoms of em all, to prevent there being Rob'd. I cannot tell you that your pidgons are Increas'd: but much the Contrary, for they are much thiner than you and I saw them last December: but I have Endevor'd to add to there Number by a philter (which you remember) and I hope it will have its effect. . . . Your new Walke and the pale to ffence it in has been a long Iobb, and has cost you a prety deale of money, but 'twill please, and then the money is well Laid out. . . . I thinke tis time to winde up my Course long home-spun thred for I can draw it no finer, but am
>
> Sr.
>
> your most obedient
>
> and most humble servant . . .

Had Addison's ambitions been bounded by those pleasant worries, had he been content to breed fatter pigeons and more enormous pike, to watch his seedlings grow to saplings, and his saplings rise to tall young trees,

BILTON HALL, CIRCA 1821

how happy he might have been—the perfect eighteenth-century man of letters. About 1715, however, he made the fatal mistake of doing something that no one had asked him to do. He fell in love with the Countess of Warwick. The expression is perhaps too strong: Addison appears to have waded in up to his knees, or a little higher. The affair, at all events, can hardly have been sudden; it seems to have been of that type, apparently so common in the next century, in which "friendship gradually ripens into love." Old Jacob Tonson, the bookseller, gave it out that Addison had thoughts of getting this lady from his very first acquaintance with the family; but Tonson disliked him, and in any case the old bookseller must have been guessing rather than stating something that he actually knew. Addison had certainly known the Countess for many years; he was, in fact, an old friend of the family, and had taken a considerable interest in the education of her only son, the young Earl of Warwick. Three of the letters written by Addison to this nobleman when he was a little boy have been preserved. In one of them particularly he displays all his natural delicacy and unemphatic wit.

My Dearest Lord,

I can't forbear being troublesome to your Lordship whilst I am in your neighbourhood. The business of this is to invite you to a concert of music, which I have found out in a neighbouring wood. It begins precisely at six in the evening, and consists of a blackbird, a thrush, a robin redbreast, and a bull-finch. There is a lark, that, by way of overture, sings and mounts till she is almost out of hearing; and afterwards, falling down leisurely, drops to the ground, or as soon as she has ended her song. The whole is concluded by a nightingale, that has a much better voice than Mrs. Tofts, and something of the Italian manner in her divisions. If your Lordship will honour me with your company, I will promise to entertain you with much better music, and more agreeable scenes, than you ever met with at the opera; and will conclude with a charming description of a nightingale, out of our friend Virgil—

Qualis populea moerens Philomela sub umbra. . . .

Your Lordship's most obedient,
J. ADDISON.

In so far as Addison was responsible for moulding the character of this young man, the Earl of Warwick was one of his failures; but he was working with poor material. The young Earl grew up to be a complete roué, and he seems to have been in every respect devoid of Addison's good qualities.

Of the Countess, his mother, few details have come down, and those are almost all to her disadvantage. She is usually described as proud and arrogant, a lady of small understanding, who consented at last to marry the commoner who had wooed her so respectfully, but who never allowed him to forget the difference in their ranks. She herself was the daughter of Sir Thomas Myddelton of Chirk, and she had become the wife of the sixth Earl of Warwick, a wild and erratic young man who left her a widow in 1701. All through the reign of Queen Anne she remained a widow, and when Addison's serious courtship began her first husband had been dead for almost fifteen years. It has been so universally assumed that she was the wrong woman for Addison that it is only fair to reproduce the portrait of her in a blue dress by Kneller, in which, as one nineteenth-century critic pointed out, she appears "decidedly handsome, . . . with a sweet expression of countenance."

Almost all Addison's biographers have hinted that after her second marriage the expression of the Countess was far from being uniformly sweet, and that her husband led a dog's life with his grand lady; but such stories may easily have been exaggerated. Biography turns only too often upon hearsay, and hearsay is frequently no more than a dramatisation of what men expect to happen. In Addison's case they expected that the clergyman's son marrying the widow of an earl could not possibly hope for happiness, that he must infallibly be miserable; and unless the marriage turned out to be a superlatively happy one it was natural that a legend of his matrimonial wretchedness should grow up and flourish in the eighteenth century. It must be confessed, however, that such evidence as is available almost all goes to suggest that on this occasion the gossips were right about the Countess, and that Kneller's portrait lied. He was, after all, a Court painter.

The state of Addison's heart was no secret to the Town, and the progress of his courtship was followed with considerable interest. When he was leaving for Ireland in 1716, Nicholas Rowe, the poet laureate, addressed some stanzas to the Countess. It is significant, perhaps, that he was less concerned to offer consolation to the lady on the departure of her lover than to plead rather anxiously with her not to forget her absent Lycidas:

> When Crowds of youthful Lovers round thee wait,
> And tender Thoughts in sweetest Words impart;
> When thou art woo'd by Titles, Wealth, and State,
> Then think on Lycidas, and guard thy Heart.
>
> When the gay Theatre shall charm thy Eyes,
> When artful Wit shall speak thy Beauty's Praise;
> When Harmony shall thy soft Soul surprise,
> Sooth all thy Senses, and thy Passions raise:
>
> Amidst whatever various Joys appear,
> Yet breathe one Sigh, for one sad Minute mourn;
> Nor let thy Heart know one Delight sincere,
> Till thy own truest Lycidas Return.

Addison, however, managed to carry it off. He married his Countess, and went to live with her in the magnificent London residence of the Warwick family, Holland House. If he was not about to experience the "fierce light which beats upon a throne," he was certainly to be embarrassed by the very considerable glitter that plays about an earldom. How much and how long he and his lady were in love with each other it would be impertinent to inquire; but that the Countess retained her sense of proportion is suggested by the fact that she got her husband to transfer £4000 to her estate, in compensation for some property which she lost if she married again. The Countess had not done badly for herself. True, her second husband was only a commoner; but he had his estate at Bilton, he drew a considerable income from various offices, and among commoners he was very nearly the most distinguished commoner in England. Besides, she had arrived at an age when someone like Addison was undeniably attractive to a lonely woman. Her son was almost a grown man, and in spite of the crowds of youthful lovers which the courtly laureate imagined for her, the Countess was in some danger of facing a cheerless and solitary old age. Addison would at least be a man about the vast and echoing halls of Holland House. And, of course, in spite of the gossip of her contemporaries, she may have been genuinely fond of him.

The Countess, indeed, had little to lose by the match; it is rather for Addison that a contemporary onlooker must have feared. For the last twenty years he had been living in rooms, rising when he pleased and going to bed when he pleased, reading, writing, poking the fire, looking out of the window, and, when he felt hungry, putting on his wig and stepping down the street to dine with his friends at an ordinary. A fillet of veal was what Addison liked best, and his bottle. Under the influence of the wine his habitual reserve would gradually melt away, and he would talk to his intimate friends in the most charming way imaginable. But the appearance of a stranger in his little company was almost certain to shut the sluice upon this delightful flow, and he would relapse into "a stiff sort of silence." This shy nocturnal creature would bolt down his hole, and the stranger would take himself off again, wondering what they all saw in this fellow who sat there so mum, "like a parson in a tie-wig." His chief companions before he married Lady Warwick were Steele, Budgell, Ambrose Philips, Carey, Davenant, and Colonel Brett. "He used to breakfast with one or other of them, at his lodgings in St. James's Place, dine at taverns with them, then to Button's, and then to some tavern again for supper in the evening: and this was the usual round of his life." A pleasant sort of life it was, too, but a poor preparation for the formal entertainments of Holland House, where the timid host might have to cope, not with one stranger, but with a whole roomful of them. Addison, indeed, belonged to that well-known class of bachelors, who, like Shaw's pathetic Tavy, live in comfortable lodgings, "and are adored by their landladies, and never get married." There was something of the unicorn about Addison, delicate, high-stepping, and remote. And now those easy informal days, and those friendly and rather maudlin nights were over; he had stiffened into a husband, and he sat opposite the Countess in the dining-room at Holland House where previously he had sat only as an honoured guest. But a man of forty-five cannot be expected to adapt himself all at once to the punctual rhythms of married life; and it is hardly surprising to learn from the poet Young that Addison used often to slip away from his grand dining-room to a coffee-house in Kensington, and there enjoy with a friend his favourite fillet and a bottle.

In April, 1717, rather more than six months after his marriage, he placed a still greater barrier between himself and his old mode of life. This time the change was not of his own making; he allowed himself to be persuaded into accepting one of the highest of all government offices, and became one of the Secretaries of State. According to Jacob Tonson, he accepted this high office to oblige the Countess, "and to qualify himself to be owned for her husband." From the point of view of the Ministry the appointment had much to recommend it, for Addison was a popular figure and would lend some of his popularity to the Government; on the other hand, he could be counted upon not to interfere with the policy of his more masterful colleagues. But in the House he was almost quite useless to the party. All the years that he had been in Parliament he could never bring himself to make a speech. Once, it is said, he was seen struggling to his feet; but the buzz of expectation was so great, and so alarming to this timid politician, that he sat down again in confusion. Pamphlets and periodicals, yes; but to stand up in a public assembly and address his fellow-members was more than he could do. His silence was forgiven him; but what proved even more embarrassing—and certainly more surprising—was his inability to write the letters required in the ordinary routine of business. While he was searching for the natural opening, the just epithet, the perfect period, the minutes were slipping away, and the King's business remained untransacted. "Mr. Addison," said Pope, "could not give out a common order in writing from his always endeavouring to word it too finely. He had too beautiful an imagination for a man of business." If Dr. Johnson's natural tendency was to make his little fishes talk like whales, Addison's inclination was to make them shine like goldfish. Three years before, when he was Secretary to the Lords of the Regency, it was his business to inform the Court of Hanover that Queen Anne was dead. The Queen of England dead! The occasion was altogether too much for Addison; he could have put his thoughts and feelings into an ode or an elegy, but his present problem was to put the bare facts into official prose. The words refused to come, or at any rate words which seemed to Addison sufficiently dignified to impart this historic news to the Court of Hanover. Meanwhile the Lords of the Regency were waiting, and at last they could wait no longer; one of the clerks—less imaginative, no doubt, but unhesitatingly competent—was summoned to write in the ordinary office style what the Secretary was unsuccessfully trying to express in perfect Addisonian English.

As Secretary of State Addison was a failure. None of the various political offices he had held in previous years had demanded the executive abilities which his new post required. Addison struggled with his unfamiliar responsibilities, but his delicate, discriminating mind was unfitted for sudden decisions and the rapid discharge of business. Writing to Pope soon after his appointment, Lady Mary Wortley Montagu made an ominous forecast:

> I received the news of Mr. Addison's being declared Secretary of State with the less surprise, in that I know that post was almost offered to him before. At that time he declined it, and I really believe that he would have done well to have declined it now. Such a post as that, and such a wife as the Countess, do not seem to be in prudence eligible for a man that is asthmatic; and we may see the day when he will be heartily glad to resign them both.

Of his asthma we are to hear more and more as the days go by. It is probable, indeed, that he was a sick man all the time that he held the secretaryship, and most of the time that he was a husband. During the year 1717 his health went steadily from bad to worse; it was becoming obvious that he had only a short time left to live. For many years he had been a heavy drinker, and his natural fondness for the bottle was probably encouraged by his friends, who knew how wine could unseal his lips. There is no evidence that he ever took the least exercise, unless it was to walk to the coffee-house or his office, or to stroll beneath his trees at Bilton; but in this he was like most Londoners of his day. Of the literary men who were Addison's contemporaries, a surprisingly large number went off in their forties or even earlier, their bodies worn out, one suspects, by excessive eating and drinking. Swift, who really worried himself about getting proper exercise, and who would walk for that very reason from the City out to Chelsea, or throw off his clothes and swim in the River, or even, in desperation, run violently up and down stairs, lived to be seventy-eight. It is unlikely, however, that Addison had run more than a few paces since he was a schoolboy; and at forty-five he was beginning to pay the penalty for a life of physical inaction. And now when his health was failing him, he began—or so they said—to take to drams; the sick man was making a last effort to cope with the day's business. By the winter of 1717 he was in a desperate state. An apoplectic fit in December nearly carried him off, and a rumour did actually get about the Town that he was dead. He recovered, however, after being bled; but so much was he weakened by dropsy, asthma, and a complication of disorders that no one expected him to last much longer.

On May 14 he resigned his secretaryship, and retired with a pension of £1700. Six days later he was writing to Swift in a fairly cheerful vein, telling him that he was now entirely free both of his office and his asthma ; but if Lady Mary had seen this letter she would no doubt have remarked that he still had the Countess.

Released from the cares of state business, and with his health now partially restored to him, Addison again began to think again of writing. He had at least two works in hand, one a *Defence of the Christian Religion*, and the other a tragedy on the death of Socrates. Tonson, ever ready to believe the worst, told Pope that after Addison had resigned his secretaryship he intended to apply for orders and obtain a bishopric, and Pope therefore assumed that those final literary labours of Addison's were intended as his passport into the Church. They are much more likely to have been the natural concern of one who was already becoming very conscious of mortality ; he did not live, in fact, to complete either. There was one other work, however, that he did live to see completed. On January 30, 1719, the Countess of Warwick became a mother, and her ailing husband a father : from those black and sooty boughs fresh green life was springing. Into this world of asthma and dropsy, of water-drinking and broken guts, there had come a baby daughter. One thinks of Addison less easily as the parent than as the perfect eighteenth-century uncle ; but had he lived long enough to watch this little girl grow up, our literature might have been enriched by a polite and graceful series of Letters to a Daughter. Addison would have done them perfectly ; they would certainly have become a domestic classic in the nineteenth century—consummately expressed, and no doubt quite useless.

The summer of 1718 he had spent at Bristol, drinking the waters there and hoping for the best. But there was no hope for him now. According to the Earl of Egmont, who had it from Charles Lillie, the perfumer, an old friend of Addison's, the last verses he ever wrote were four unhappy lines in which he expressed his weariness with life :

> Plagued by a vexatious wife,
> And tired of this packhorse life,
> I'll to the stable hie
> And slip my pack, and die.

It is just possible that Addison did write those lines ; they sound like the lines a man might write in a tavern some time after midnight when his drink was not agreeing with him. The Countess may have been unusually exacting, and Addison may have flung out of the house, and proceeded to get fuddled in his favourite tavern. But they display a very different frame of mind from that in which he finally took leave of his life, when in June, 1719, he lay on his death-bed at Holland House.

The closing scenes of Addison's life belong peculiarly to the eighteenth century. As his strength ebbed away, he seems to have set about the business of dying with a classical composure. A fortnight before the end, he summoned his old friend Gay to Holland House, and begged his forgiveness—though what it was that he wanted him to forgive Gay never discovered. But the grandest scene of all was reserved for the final curtain. Addison had been doing good all his life, preaching so pleasantly at his contemporaries that they hardly realised he was entertaining them with sermons, and now he saw a chance of turning even his death to good account. He had to die, but his death could be made to yield a lesson. Was his mind running upon that unfinished tragedy of his on the death of Socrates—Plato's and Xenophon's Socrates, who died so easily and with such exemplary calm, demonstrating up to his very last breath the fortitude with which a true philosopher could meet his end? It was an age of imitation; the men of letters were never so happy as when they were following the best classical models. At all events, Addison remembered his wild and heedless stepson, the young Earl of Warwick, and sent for him. What actually happened in those last moments remained a secret until almost exactly forty years later; and then at length the poet Young disclosed the facts for the edification of the public. Addison, says Young, would have deserved immortality even if he had never written a line; for he left behind him an example too striking to be forgotten. The young Earl was brought to the bedside of the dying man, and, after a decent and proper pause, spoke to him . . . "Dear Sir! you sent for me. I believe, and I hope, that you have some commands; I shall hold them most sacred." Addison grasped the hand of his stepson: "See in what peace a Christian can die!" he said softly, and soon afterwards he expired. "Who would not thus expire?" adds Young, on whose own theatrical nature such a scene must have made a deep impression. What effect this little drama had upon the dissipated Earl, Young does not tell us, for his whole attention is given to the effect that it ought to have upon posterity; but Addison's dying gesture seems to have made no permanent impression upon his stepson, for just over two years later the young man followed him to the grave, having killed himself, according to one of his contemporaries, with his debauchery.

It is more relevant, perhaps, to consider what the scene must have meant to Addison himself. When some one spoke in the presence of Dr. Johnson against public executions, the great man rounded on him with characteristic sense. It was argued that the new practice of hanging criminals behind the prison walls was an improvement. "No, Sir (said he, eagerly), it is *not* an improvement; they object, that the old method drew together a number of spectators. Sir, executions are intended to draw spectators. If they do not draw spectators, they don't answer their purpose. The old method was most satisfactory to all parties; the publick was gratified by a procession; the criminal was supported by it. Why is all this to be swept away?" Certainly from the point of view of the criminal there is much to be said in favour of public execution; and for the dying man there may be real support and consolation in playing the closing scene of his own drama before a suitably impressed audience. And so as Addison lay there in the great bedchamber in Holland House, breathing out his last in the presence of the faltering Earl, the drama of the thing may have sustained him and eased the grim parting of soul from body. Nor can one grudge him his pious scene; there had been too little drama in the life of Addison.

CURRENT INTELLIGENCE

1709–1710

Never Acted before. At the Theatre Royal, in Drury-Lane, to Morrow being Tuesday, will be presented, A New Comedy, call'd The Modern Prophets.

Yesterday the Sessions ended at the Old Bailey, where Eight Men receiv'd Sentence of Death for Murder, Burglaries, and Robberies.

We have fought the most glorious and the most bloody Battle[1] *that has been known for many Ages. . . . 'Tis computed that we had in the late Battle 12 or 13,000 Men kill'd and wounded, and the French above 20,000. . . . The French have had Two Days allow'd them to bury their Dead, and carry off their wounded Men upon Parole.*

Deserted from Sir Cha. Hotham's Regiment, Edw. Burton, about 5 Foot 10 Inches, mark'd with the small Pox, a light Wigg, Lac'd Hat and gilt hilted Sword. . . .

Yesterday the Great Guns of the Tower were fired upon account of the Success of the Confederate Army in passing the Lines in Flanders.

Mr. Ford of Kensington who removes Impediments of the Speech, such as Snufling, Stammering, etc. . . .

The Duke of Marlborough's Army encamp'd with the Right at Vitry, that of Prince Eugene remaining on the other side to invest the Town between the Scarpe and the Canal.

[1] Malplaquet.

Last Night Bank Stock was 123, Million Bank 75 and a half, Sword Blades 65. . . .

Mount Vesuvius has begun to Belch out Flames and make great Roarings, which makes us fearful of an Irruption.

For the Entertainment of the Four Indian Kings lately arriv'd in this Kingdom will be seen the Royal Sport of Cock-fighting for 2 Guineas a Battle. . . .

Bohee Tea, 16s. a Pound.

Miss Addison

A Maid whom there were none to praise
And very few to love.

W. Wordsworth

THE children of a great man are something of an irrelevance, less significant to posterity than the clothes he wore and the books he read ; if they tell us anything, it is generally only what the great man would have been like if he had not been great. Certain stubborn physical traits, a dominant nose on the female side, an early morning cough from the father, are handed on in unfailing succession ; but the great man seems to be a natural freak, unable to transmit more than the normal family attributes to his progeny. It is customary, at any rate, for the world to be disappointed in the sons and daughters of the illustrious, and to marvel how such remarkable personalities should have been cursed with so feeble an offspring. Perhaps the world expects too much, and is too ready, when the second generation reverts to the normal strain, to describe it as degenerate. Something of this sort seems to have happened with the daughter of Joseph Addison.

Born on January 30, 1719, only a few months before her father died, Charlotte Addison lived very nearly long enough to see the century out ; but in all those years she gave no indication, either in conduct or character, that she had inherited any of his good qualities. She was, in fact, a great disappointment to everyone—even, one fears, to herself. There were two or three exciting years when she was still new to the world and young and tolerably pretty, when she sat flirting her fan in London drawing-rooms, and young men crowded into her box at the theatre, and handed her to her coach; but those bright, glittering prospects passed away and she settled down to being an unmarried lady. She had a house in Town and an estate in the country, she had nearly £20,000 in the funds, she was willing enough to get a husband; and yet she died an old maid. Life which had swirled so gaily round the young heiress of seventeen gradually drew away its tides, and left her stranded in a silent old house in Warwickshire, receiving the parson's visits, listening to the statements of her steward, and growing older every year with her chairs and bed-covers, her coach and her horses, her pigeon-house and gates and fences and fish-ponds. Why did she never bring a husband to Bilton, even if it was only a parson or a small impoverished squire? Was she too hard to please? Or did she never tell her love? Or did some handsome young fellow love her, and then forget her?

The truth about Charlotte Addison seems to be altogether less romantic. While she was still alive, rumours that she was not very clever began to get into print. "Indeed, by all accounts," wrote a certain facetious pamphleteer, "she was not a Minerva from the brain of Jupiter." All the evidence points to an old age of mental decay; but many a strong-minded lady begins to grow a little eccentric in her seventies, and still more so in her eighties. Perhaps Miss Addison's wits only began to fail her when she was quite an old lady? The eighteenth century would not have it so. A "very respectable lady," who was educated at the same boarding-school as Addison's daughter, reported that she was distinguished at school "by her marked dislike to his writings, and unconquerable aversion to the perusal of them." This grave circumstance was obviously cited to put her stupidity beyond all reasonable doubt; but whatever the eighteenth century may have thought of a daughter who showed an unconquerable aversion to her father's writings, the twentieth is apt to be more indulgent, and even to see in her unfilial boredom a clear indication of intelligence. In her own day, however, the tradition of her stupidity was too positive to be ignored; and no sooner was she dead than a correspondent of the *Gentleman's Magazine* stated that she had been little better than an imbecile. This statement drew a warm protest from another correspondent two months later: Miss Addison's understanding was perhaps a little clouded occasionally, but never for long at a time. Moreover, she had some positive accomplishments: she spoke French, for instance, and "a person who had opportunities of observing" was willing to testify that she spelt it with some correctness.

Few kinds of scandal grow more quickly than the sort which whispers that Miss A. is a little—*you* know—not quite right in her head. Once this kind of rumour has started, there is no stopping it. Poor Miss Addison had cheated expectation: she was no Minerva, she had failed to keep up the tradition. But was there anything more in it than that? A little; but not nearly so much as the gossips would have liked to believe. There is good evidence that however much she may have deteriorated in her old age, she was no more than ordinarily stupid in her youth. A flighty, undisciplined, empty-headed girl, she gave her guardians a great deal of anxiety; but when she reached the age of twenty-one there was no suggestion of protecting her from herself, or preventing her from managing her own affairs. If she was no Minerva, neither was she an imbecile. So much justice it is possible to do her; but having said that, one can say little more in praise of Charlotte Addison. She was—and there is no escaping it—a sad disappointment.

When Addison was carried to Westminster Abbey, and put away among the other illustrious ones, he left his baby daughter in charge of a mother whose only other attempt at bringing up a child had been a startling failure. The young Earl of Warwick was just arriving at manhood, and it was already quite clear that he was going to turn out a hopeless rake. Addison may have taught him how a Christian could die, but no one had been able to teach the young man how he should live. He had inherited bad blood from his father, however, and the fault may not have been in his upbringing: Charlotte, on the other hand, was half an Addison, and a child of sober middle age, if that counts for anything. Like the children of other rich parents in the eighteenth century, she grew up partly in the Town, and partly in the country. In the winter the Countess opened her house in London, receiving visits and entertaining her friends; in the summer, when the Court moved out of Town, and the streets grew hot and dusty, and the theatres were closed, the Countess shut up her house again and went down to Bilton. Here little Miss Addison could ride her pony, and talk to old Walker, the factor, a favourite of hers, and run about with far more freedom than was possible in the big London house with its tall windows and its long stairs and its stiff powdered footmen. Here, too, she had her own room, with its seven Dutch chairs, and its sixteen Indian pictures, and its own special bed—"Miss Addison's little bed," as the inventory men called it when her mother died, and they came to Bilton to take stock of the furniture. And if she had a mind to go exploring in the house, there was the Blue Bed Chamber to peep into, and the Yellow Bed Chamber, and the Red Damask Bed Chamber, and the Sprigged Bed Chamber, and the Calico Bed Chamber ; and there was the Long Passage, with its seven maps hanging upon the walls, and (most impressive of all) the Drawing-Room, with its two Japanese settees covered in yellow, its black tea-table, its seven whole-length portraits in their gilt frames, and the large picture of the Holy Family. It was a big, rambling house, the oldest part dating from the early seventeenth century ; Addison had modernised it, and he had given a great deal of thought to the garden, laying out the grounds with straight walks and plantations of young trees.

How much love and affection the Countess had for her little daughter it is impossible to tell ; but there was always Aunt Combes, Addison's sister, and with her she was on defiantly intimate terms some years later, to the annoyance of her guardians. There were other and grander relations of her mother's, and no doubt the little girl was made much of by formidable ladies in rustling silk who remarked with astonishment what a big girl she was growing ; but of all this, as nothing is known, it is perhaps best to say nothing. When she had reached the necessary age, she was sent to school, and hated it. It was not merely that her insensitiveness to the beauties of Addison's prose was paralleled in her other studies : Charlotte was too timid and excitable to enjoy school life. At present, however, she had to do what she was told ; and so she had to learn her lessons with the other children of quality, and wait miserably till the summer came round again and she could go back again to Bilton.

And then, quite unexpectedly, the Countess died. She had lived long enough to guide Addison's daughter into her thirteenth year, and she had taken proper steps to safeguard the child's future by appointing four guardians to look after her until she should reach her majority. For the next eight years those four gentlemen had to wrestle with a number of difficult and occasionally exasperating problems. They took their responsibilities seriously, and endeavoured in their different ways to carry out the Countess's wishes; but they were only men after all, very rarely all together in the same place at the same time, and in their efforts to do what they considered best for their ward they tended to cancel each other out. Worst of all, they had to deal with a giddy and mercurial girl, whose inclinations were seldom the same for two days on end.

The choice of the Countess had fallen upon the Earl of Cholmondeley, Sir John Bridgeman, Bart., the Hon. John Dawnay, and Mr. Justice Denton. Of the four, the Earl of Cholmondeley was easily the most important in the eyes of the world. So important was he, indeed, that Mr. Dawnay never thought of differing from his opinion. George, second Earl of Cholmondeley,[1] was a distinguished soldier; he had commanded the Horse-Grenadier Guards at the Battle of the Boyne, and had fought bravely at the Battle of Steinkirk, where he was wounded. Honours had followed, and he had been made a General of the Horse, Governor of Guernsey, Lord-Lieutenant and Custos Rotulorum of Chester and North Wales. Apart from his military achievements, he was also a person of intelligence; a Fellow of the Royal Society, and apparently something of a poet in

[1] He succeeded his brother in 1725.

his early years. He was the oldest of the four guardians, close upon seventy, and his health was fast breaking up ; but as long as he lived he continued to give Charlotte Addison's affairs a good deal of his attention, and to some extent to dominate the situation.

Mr. Dawnay, the youngest of the four, and, like Shakespeare's Lepidus, a rather slight, unmeritable man, had sat as Member of Parliament for Pontefract some years before, but he had not distinguished himself in any way. The Earl of Egmont, who knew him well, was more impressed by his piety than his brains. He read prayers to his servants twice a day, he was a most regular churchgoer, he was a kind father. But when you had said that, you had said almost all that you could for Mr. Dawnay. " He has just parts enough," the Earl noted in his diary, " not to be distinguished for the want of them." Such distinction as he possessed was inherited, for he was the son of Viscount Downe. Some day, perhaps, he would succeed to the title and become the third Viscount, but at present he was no more than the Hon. John Dawnay, and his father was in excellent health. Poor Mr. Dawnay never did, in fact, become Viscount ; his father took much better care of himself than most gentlemen were accustomed to do in the eighteenth century, and lived on to be seventy-six, several months too long for his son, who died rather less than a year before him. As soon as he became a guardian Dawnay fell into step with General Cholmondeley ; and after the General had died he continued to march—though not very decisively—along the road that the General would presumably have taken if he had still been there.

General Cholmondeley was competent enough at his own business of fighting ; but as a guardian he had the misfortune to be dealing, not with a troop of soldiers, but with a single irresponsible girl. It was Mr. Justice Denton who showed the best understanding of Charlotte Addison. If the General was too ready to bring the child up on general principles which he would have been prepared to apply to any female ward he had to deal with, the Judge was well aware that this particular ward was likely to need very careful and individual handling. Left to the General and Mr. Dawnay, Charlotte Addison's life might have been miserable indeed. The two men would almost certainly have tried to turn her into a fine lady, and it is to the credit of the Judge that he realised almost from the first that such a thing was quite impossible. Alexander Denton, who was fifty when the Countess died, was a lawyer of real ability. He was descended from an old Buckinghamshire family, and he had sat as Member of Parliament for both the town and the county. In 1722 he had been made a Justice of the Common Pleas, and he would almost certainly have become Lord Chief Justice some years later if Sir Robert Walpole had not blocked his progress.[1] As far as substance went, he was probably better off than Mr. Dawnay—or, for that matter, than the General—for he had married a lady who brought him twenty thousand pounds. He was undoubtedly the ablest of the four guardians; but his frequent absences from London when he went on circuit prevented him from attending to his ward's business as promptly as he might

[1] The Earl of Egmont's account of what happened may or may not be correct: "When the Chief Justice's place of the Common Pleas was last vacant, there were two that put in for it, Judge Denton, and Sir John Willes. Denton exposed his long service, to which Sir Robert Walpole replied: 'I confess it, but you don't whore; Willes must have it.' 'I did not know,' answered Denton, 'that whoring is a necessary qualification for a Chief Justice,' and going his way made no scruple to relate the story."—*Diary of the Earl of Egmont,* vol. iii, p. 270.

otherwise have done. Without his experience and his common sense, however, Charlotte Addison's prospects of happiness would have been far smaller than they were.

The fourth guardian, Sir John Bridgeman of Castle Bromwich in Warwickshire, was a charming old man. He was a year or two younger than the General, but well advanced in life, as he rarely failed to remind his correspondents. Fortunately he was an orderly old gentleman; and it is his habit of filing his correspondence with the other three guardians that has made it possible to follow the fortunes of Addison's daughter up to her twenty-first birthday.[1] As a guardian he was conscientious rather than competent; and if Mr. Dawnay was little more than an echo of the General, Sir John was apt on all important decisions to fall in behind the Judge. He seems to have had no liking for London; and as he preferred to remain at Castle Bromwich even in the winter, Charlotte Addison's affairs involved him and his fellow-guardians in a good deal of correspondence. Faced with the task of writing a letter, Sir John generally drafted it out (sometimes more than once) in his crabbed handwriting before sending off a fair copy to his correspondent. But though the handwriting is painstaking, and the sentiments are often naïvely expressed, he was clearly a sensible man, able to make sound judgments about the men and women with whom he had to deal, modest and efficient in his own sphere. In some ways, too, he was the most important of Charlotte's guardians, for he was related to her on her mother's side.[2] In his letters he invariably addressed her as "Dear Cosen," and though he necessarily saw nothing of her when she was in London, he could, and he did, invite

[1] The correspondence is preserved in the British Museum: Egerton MSS. 1974.

[2] Sir John and the Countess were first cousins.

her to stay with him at Castle Bromwich, and he encouraged his women folk to visit her at Bilton. Charlotte was obviously grateful to the old man, and in her letters she was accustomed to address him with all the deference and humility that even an eighteenth-century baronet could expect.

The guardians lost no time in setting about their business. The day after the Countess's death Mr. Justice Denton wrote to Sir John, to inform him that he had been appointed one of her executors and trustees. Sir John sat down at once and wrote a kind letter to his little cousin: he would have come to see her if he had not been suffering from a fever, but she might depend upon it that she would always be very welcome at Castle Bromwich. A few days later Mr. Denton wrote again. Lady Warwick had once told him that her daughter would be worth forty thousand pounds, but he now thinks that she must have put the figure too high. He has found about a thousand pounds in cash, and there is probably another twelve thousand or so in the stocks; and of course there is Bilton. At any rate the child is something of an heiress. Meanwhile Charlotte, now in her thirteenth year, was spending the winter in London. "Miss Addison is in perfect health," the Judge wrote on December 8, 1731, "& grows very tall." Old Walker had come up from Bilton in November to pay her a visit, and he wrote to Sir John to say that young Miss sent him her services.

So far everything had worked out smoothly; but now a split began to appear between the Judge and the General, and as General Cholmondeley had obviously got a complete ascendancy over Mr. Dawnay, the Judge hastened to write to Sir John, in the hope of bringing him over to his side. By a codicil to her will the Countess

CHARLOTTE ADDISON AS A CHILD

had expressed a wish that her daughter should leave school in January, 1732, when she would be entering upon her fourteenth year, and should then be entrusted to the care of a certain Mrs. Crofts. The General did not think much of this idea, believing that it would be better for her to stay on at school for some time longer; and Mr. Dawnay, of course, thought the same. Mr. Denton, on the contrary, believed that the Countess was right, and that her wishes should be respected; she knew her own daughter better than anyone else could be expected to do, and she had picked out Mrs. Crofts as the person most likely to improve the child's mind and character. "We ought not to consider of means to enlarge her fortune," he wrote to Sir John, "but rather to study how her mind may be improved, and her conduct well regulated." Mrs. Crofts, he was convinced, was an admirable choice; she was much in demand among the nobility, and had educated the Marquess of Wharton's two daughters, the Lady Jane and the Lady Lucy. But for the present the Judge was not allowed to have things his own way; the General was still a fighting force, and with Mr. Dawnay in support he could bring two against the Judge's two, if, indeed, he did not manage to win over Sir John and make it three to one. If the Countess had selected her four guardians so as to avoid the danger of any one of them dictating to the rest what her daughter's future should be, she could not have been more successful: after a few months of endeavouring to work together the four men had come to a complete deadlock. Sir John, in fact, had decided to cast his vote on the side of the Judge. "I shall always have a great regard to your advice," he wrote, "and esteem it a great pleasure to joyn with you in whatever will be for the interest we are intrusted with." So now there were two guardians in favour of Charlotte's continuing at school, and two opposed to it ; and the split was rapidly becoming a breach.

In those trying circumstances the guardians (or, more accurately perhaps, General Cholmondeley and Mr. Justice Denton) decided that the only course to adopt was to refer the matter to the Lord Chancellor for a decision. Were they, in fact, to stand by the codicil to Lady Warwick's will and place her daughter under the care of Mrs. Crofts, or were they entitled to ignore the will and act as they thought best? The Lord Chancellor deliberated, and in due course gave his decision : the trustees were at liberty to act as they thought best, notwithstanding the codicil. The General and Mr. Dawnay had won the preliminary skirmish ; but it was only a hollow victory, since the Lord Chancellor had given them nothing more than the right to set aside the codicil, if the other two guardians agreed. The Judge stood firm, and behind him stood Sir John ; but the General must have carried his point, for Charlotte remained at school. He was annoyed, however, to have only Mr. Dawnay supporting him. In September, 1732, he wrote rather peevishly to Castle Bromwich, telling Sir John in so many words that he was allowing himself to be overruled by Judge Denton. Sir John was polite, as befitted a baronet addressing an Earl, but he stood by the Judge. He would always, he explained, have a due preference for his Lordship's judgment ; but before he could give his consent to allowing Miss Addison to be educated in a different method from what Lady Warwick had thought proper to direct, he would require very good reasons. How long did his Lordship think of keeping Miss at school? If they did not remove her very soon they would lose Mrs. Crofts, who would naturally dispose of herself to some other family, since she could not be expected to hold herself in readiness indefinitely. To this letter the General apparently made no reply, or if he did, Sir John did not file it with the rest. There were good reasons why the General should be peevish, for his health was rapidly growing worse. As early as June there had been an ominous reference in one of the Judge's letters to a fit of the palsy that had shaken the old soldier considerably, and at the beginning of 1733 he was taken ill again. On May 7 he was dead.

The number of Charlotte's guardians had now dropped to three, and two of those were in complete agreement. True, there was still Mr. Dawnay left to make difficulties, but though he might be troublesome he was not formidable. On May 16 old Walker wrote to Sir John from Bilton; he had been hoping that the guardians would send Miss to live at Bilton, and now he saw some chance of his hopes being realised.

"Miss Addison I heare is Ille of ye measols," he wrote,

> but I wish hit be not something wors for shee hade the measols fore or five yeares agoe. I wish they Doe not Keep her In town till shee Looses hir Life but I hope your honour will youse your Intrest for hir Coming to bilton for the Case Is alterd now, for now I hope their Is two to one for hir Coming Into ye Cuntry.

Apparently it was not the "measols" that the young lady was suffering from, for the next day she was reported to be better, and her doctor had ordered her to Kensington to take the air. Meanwhile Mr. Denton had his own troubles to bear; his wife had been seriously ill for some time, and in July he wrote to Sir John to say that she was dead. Sir John had invited their ward to pass the summer with him at Castle Bromwich, and the Judge was very willing that she should do so. The girl had the strongest aversion to going back to school, and she had such weak nerves that, in the opinion of the Judge, " the very apprehension of it may put her into fits." So Charlotte went to spend the summer with Sir John and his family in the country, stopping one night at Bilton on her way. "We could not," the Judge explained, " without a disappointment dissuade her from it."

At Castle Bromwich she remained for almost a year. Sir John wrote in September to say that he had been sounding Miss about her going back to school, and had found that she had no inclination to return. He suggested accordingly that they should try to find " some discreet, ingenious, and faithfull person that will constantly be with her on all occasions." Unfortunately Mrs. Crofts was no longer available, for she had entered the service of Lady Carlisle ; it was a great pity that they had lost her, since Miss had a liking for Mrs. Crofts, and had been corresponding with her. The Judge agreed that Mrs. Crofts would have suited her admirably, but he did not think she would leave Lady Carlisle's family to take over Charlotte, who was rapidly growing up and could not be long under her care now.

" The loss of Mrs. Crofts," he added rather bitterly,

> is entirely owing to the perverseness of Lord Cholmondley and the influence he had over Mr. Dawnay, who was made to believe she would improve most at School, but now you have had her in your house for some time, you may easily observe she is not so fit for such an Education.

He promised to call on Mr. Dawnay as soon as he returned to London ; but he was quite sure that Mr. Dawnay would be very backward in inquiring for a suitable person to take charge of their ward. It looks, indeed, as if Dawnay had taken offence : Miss Addison was being removed from school against his advice, and if Mr. Denton thought that someone ought to be put in charge of her it was his business to find such a person.

Towards the middle of October, however, the two guardians in London were in a sufficiently amicable frame of mind to send a joint letter to Sir John, thanking him for keeping Miss at Castle Bromwich, and asking him to let her stay there till the following summer. The old baronet replied that she was welcome to stay until some better arrangement could be made. Towards the end of May he wrote to remind the other two guardians that Miss was still with him at Castle Bromwich, and to ask whether they had yet found a suitable person to look after her education: she was growing up quickly, and there was no time to be lost. At last, late in June, Mr. Denton was able to tell Sir John that he and Mr. Dawnay had come to an agreement with a gentlewoman, Mrs. Mary Kellar, and she would set out for Bilton about the middle of July.

On the whole, Mrs. Kellar seems to have given satisfaction; but she did not play a very prominent part in Charlotte's life, and her name appears only once or twice in Sir John's correspondence. Perhaps she helped her new charge to write the letter of thanks which Sir John received from his young cousin after she had gone back to Bilton, or perhaps Charlotte had learnt something at school after all. At any rate the letter concluded with a correctly turned sentiment that must have met with the old gentleman's complete approval: "A few lines that brings me the good news of your Health will be a very great Satisfaction to, Sir, your most Dutiful and Obedient Servant, C. Addison."

Charlotte spent the next winter in London, and early

in December Sir John's sister was able to send him a favourable report about her progress. It was generally thought that she showed some improvement under Mrs. Kellar's care. "Mrs. Keelar," he read, "seems to perform her part very well and Miss is pleased wth her and observes her directions as much as can be exspected." She was growing up, too, and was now to be given an allowance of one hundred pounds a year for her clothes, her pocket money, and her amusements at Christmas.

For the next ten months Charlotte gave little cause for any further correspondence between the guardians; but on November 15, 1735, an important letter from Mr. Justice Denton arrived at Castle Bromwich. It contained nothing less than the news that a baronet's widow was prepared to enter into negotiations for a match between her son and Miss Addison. A certain Mr. Parker, "a gentleman at the Bar," had come to the Judge with a proposal from Lady Broughton, the mother of young Sir Brian Broughton, the present baronet. Sir Brian was still at Oxford, a "sober, prudent, and well-behaved young Gentleman" by all reports, and he was heir to an estate that would ultimately be worth £5000 per annum. Charlotte was still two months short of her seventeenth birthday, and though the Judge could hardly help being impressed with the offer, he thought that they were both too young to think seriously about getting married yet. Two weeks later Sir John wrote from Castle Bromwich to say that he had been making inquiries among his neighbours and had heard good reports of young Sir Brian. He was said to be "a pritty Scholar," and a sober young fellow. Of his mother he was able to report that she was of a frugal temper and "pritty positive when she has a mind of her way"—

the sort of woman, one feels, that Sir John would rather have left the Judge to deal with if the need arose.

What Charlotte thought about Sir Brian, or whether she had yet been told anything about the match, it is impossible to tell. Towards the end of March it looked as if the negotiations were likely to break down; the gentleman who made the original proposal had not repeated it, and Mr. Dawnay had heard that Sir Brian did not approve of his mother's choice for him. Meanwhile the young lady had been very ill indeed, and there were fears that she had caught the small-pox, but "being blouded yesterday she is now much better & it proves only to be a cold." The next stage in the negotiations is confusing because Mr. Dawnay appears to have acted in a disingenuous manner, deceiving the Judge, and misleading Lady Broughton. At all events Lady Broughton turned up at Castle Bromwich with her son early in June, and Sir Brian asked to be allowed to visit Miss Addison at Bilton. Either his mother's habit of getting her own way had brought them both to Castle Bromwich, or else Mr. Dawnay had been misinformed about the young man's indifference to the match, and Sir Brian was now showing a pardonable curiosity about the young lady he was expected to marry. Sir John, who, in his own words, was anxious to see his cousin "happily setled in a good family with a sober discreet gentleman," seems to have felt that Sir Brian would do very well; but either his natural timidity or a sense of loyalty to his fellow-guardians prevented him from allowing the young man to visit his ward at Bilton unless he obtained the consent of the other two. He therefore communicated Sir Brian's request to Mr. Denton.

The Judge's reply must have startled him. He was glad that Lady Broughton and her son had called at

Castle Bromwich, because Sir John would be able to judge for himself how oddly they had been treated. Lady Broughton had come to Town to discuss the match ; but shortly afterwards Charlotte had called upon him—apparently she had made a special journey to London for the purpose—and asked that no further steps should be taken in the affair until she came to Town in the winter. A little later Mr. Dawnay had seconded this request.

"I told her," the Judge explained,

> whatever steps could be made in it, it would be only conditionally that they liked each other, and she would not be pressed to it if she did not like him after she had been at a place where he was. I ask'd her if she had any dislike to him ; she answer'd no, but still insisted nothing shd be done.

After she had returned to Bilton she wrote him a letter begging him again to do nothing further in the matter at present. The Judge was convinced that there was some sort of conspiracy against the match, though why, he had no idea. Lady Broughton's offer was a very handsome one, and he believed that the girl herself had no real objection to marriage or to this particular young man. Had Mr. Dawnay some much more ambitious match in view for the young lady ?

Sir John might well be confused by all those odd goings-on. His troubles were not lessened by a letter which he received from Lady Broughton about the middle of August. She was concerned about the delays which she and her son had met with in their attempts to visit the young lady.

"Tis what Sr. Brian is very desireous of," she told him.

> I was quite uneasie w[n] he was in Town upon Acc[t] of y[e] Small-pox he not haveing had it, & therefore intreat the Country may be y[e] place of Courtship. Where persons are to pass their lifes

> together, in order to do it happyly I can't but think it nesessary they should be acquainted wth each others temper wch can't be done without being in ye House together.

Meanwhile Sir Brian sent a message to say that he was at Rugby, waiting impatiently for the decision of the trustees.

But still nothing happened; and as long as Sir John persisted in staying at Castle Bromwich for twelve months in the year and Mr. Justice Denton went off periodically on his circuit it was difficult for anything to happen at all without interminable correspondence. And even though the Judge and Sir John were in substantial agreement, Mr. Dawnay had still to be won over to their point of view. The summer passed, and the winter came, and still Sir Brian had not been granted a sight of the young lady who might one day be Lady Broughton. By this time he might be forgiven if suspicions had begun to form in his mind that the guardians must have something to conceal, or something, at least, that they were not very confident of producing. Two weeks before Christmas, however, the negotiations took a real step forward. Charlotte had apparently become reconciled to the thought of marrying the young baronet, for word reached Sir John that, as she had raised no further objections to the match, the Judge and Mr. Dawnay had now drawn up a suitable claim on her behalf for the marriage settlement. In answer to Lady Broughton's inquiries they estimated the value of their ward's stock, plate, and securities at £18,000; the estate at Bilton was worth £600 per annum, and there was also her house in Burlington Gardens. Apparently Lady Broughton was satisfied; the match had attracted her from the first, for she and Lady Warwick had been playfellows many years ago, and the marriage of their two children would have a sentimental interest for her, besides being quite satisfactory from a more worldly point of view. She must, indeed, have been "pritty positive" about having her own way before she could triumph over all the obstacles that had been rolled so persistently across her path.

At last the tedious preliminaries were settled, and one day in the spring of 1737 Sir Brian was permitted to visit his young lady. She was now in the full bloom of youth, just past her eighteenth birthday; if ever she was going to charm the heart of a young baronet she ought surely to do so now. Sir Brian came and paid his visit. He came again a second time for politeness' sake, and then he came no more. Had the long interval of waiting wound his imagination up so high that when at last he looked upon his lady her charms seemed meagre and inadequate compared to those he had taught himself to expect? Or had this "pritty scholar" from Oxford seasoned his conversation with some references to the polite writers of the age, and found his future bride insensitive to the beauties of her father's prose? Was it her mind or her face, her conversation or her deportment, that seemed to him unsuitable for the future Lady Broughton?

It was left to the family lawyer to break the news to Sir John, and it was a sad story that he had to tell. Sir Brian had behaved rather badly.

"I have it in Command from Mr. Iustice Denton," the lawyer wrote,

> to acq^{t} you that after He and Mr. Dawnay had treated with Lady Broughton for a Match between Her Son and Miss Addison, & agreed upon all matters necessary to be provided for by Settlemts the Gentleman was permitted to visit the Young Lady, wch he did twice, but having afterwards not only desisted from further Visits, but likewise dropt some expressions of his dislike in too publick a manner, the Iudge and Mr. Dawnay look upon it, as they imagine you will do, as an Affair quite at an end.

And so Sir Brian passed, not too heroically, out of Charlotte Addison's life. Almost exactly a year later he married the daughter of an M.P. He died only a few years later, in the summer of 1744.

Charlotte had now suffered a serious disappointment. Whether she really wanted Sir Brian or not, he, with the prerogative of his sex, and the cruelty of youth, had made it quite clear that he did not want her. No tradesman can enjoy watching the passer-by pause for a moment or two outside his window, and then, after a few contemptuous glances at the goods for sale, pass on again ; but when it is oneself that is for sale the experience must be doubly painful. By all the laws of human nature the next few months were likely to be dangerous ones in the life of this young lady ; and she did, in fact, give her guardians increasing cause for anxiety. From his sister, Mrs. Eyton, Sir John learnt in October that the parson at Bilton was paying Charlotte too much attention, and people were saying that it was only his modesty that prevented him from asking her hand in marriage. Mrs. Eyton was inclined to lay the blame upon Aunt Combes, who was staying with her niece at Bilton, and she suggested that Sir John should find out from Walker what actually was going on there.

Meanwhile Charlotte had been to Astrop Wells, and had met there another young gentleman who had taken a fancy to her. This one was something better than a country parson ; he was the son of Sir William Keyte, a Gloucestershire baronet worth £2500 a year. Alarmed at the Bilton rumours, Sir John wrote off to London at once ; but fortunately Mr. Denton was able to reassure him about the parson. Mr. Dawnay had inquired into the affair, and had found that the report was entirely groundless, " and did proceed from the Gent. visiting

Mrs. Combes, Miss Addison's Aunt, and that this was occasioned by his going with them in the Coach to one or two places." The Judge had also some further information about Sir William Keyte's son : it was quite true that he had met Miss Addison at Astrop Wells, and he appeared to have taken a fancy for her. "That," the Judge added with a touch of bitterness, "is not the case of every man who has a good estate."

Events were now moving rapidly. On the same day Mr. Andrews, the family lawyer, wrote to Sir John to announce that Sir William Keyte had made a proposal for the marriage of his son to Miss Addison. "The young Gentleman," the lawyer explained, "has looked with an Eye of Observation necessary for a person that intended to become a Suitor." So there would be no danger, if the match were allowed to proceed, of this young man backing out of his obligations at the last minute. Moreover, he had a good character, and was free from the common vices of the age ; and though those were qualities that might not weigh very much with the young lady, they were very important in the eyes of her guardians.

This time it was Sir John who held up the proceedings. He had been asked by the other two guardians to find out what he could about the Keytes and their estate ; but he was very slow about getting his information. In December Mr. Andrews wrote again to say that Sir William Keyte was growing impatient for his answer, and that the other two guardians were only waiting for Sir John's approval before they proceeded with the negotiations.

While Sir John was dallying in this unaccountable way, and Sir William Keyte fretting with impatience, the young lady whose future they were deciding among themselves suddenly asserted herself in an unexpected fashion. The trouble arose over Aunt Combes. Both Mr. Dawnay and the Judge had been coming to think that this middle-aged lady was having a bad influence on their ward. Swift, who had met and dined with her many years before in the company of Addison and Steele, had described her to Stella as "a sort of a wit," adding that she was very like her brother, but that he was not fond of her. At all events she was attractive enough to be twice married, once to a Prebendary of Westminster, and afterwards to Daniel Combes; and she seems to have been a woman of spirit, and a much gayer influence on young Charlotte's life than Mr. Dawnay, or the Judge, or the kindly folk at Castle Bromwich. Charlotte was undoubtedly fond of Aunt Combes, and liked her to stay at Bilton; the guardians apparently thought that she was encouraging Miss too much, and allowing—or even inviting—young men to visit her. Feeling that the time had come to assert their authority, they wrote to Charlotte at Bilton, informing her that they did not think it right that Mrs. Combes should remain there any longer. Instead of accepting the ban upon her aunt with a proper submissiveness, Charlotte came up to Town, bringing Mrs. Combes with her, and seemed to be "so farr determined not to part with her, that on Mr. Dawnay's writing her on her first comeing to Town she told him, that as he was not a friend of her Aunt's, she sho'd not for the future regard any thing he said, but apply herself to my Lord Chancellor for every thing she wanted, on which Mr. Dawnay quitted the room, and has not seen her since, nor does intend it, till she makes a proper submission for such usage." Poor Sir John did not know what to make of it all, and wrote to the Judge asking for more facts.

The reply came back that Miss Addison was behaving in a very obstinate fashion, and was quite determined to stick to Mrs. Combes; she had already informed Mrs. Kellar that she would not go down to the country unless her aunt was allowed to accompany her. The Judge had not seen the young lady herself, but he understood that she was willing to submit to her guardians in other matters if only she was allowed to keep her aunt. He himself took a gloomy view of the situation, and for the girl's own good he was inclined to compromise; the great thing was to get her married as soon as possible, or worse might follow. "It is to be feared," he concluded ominously, "if we cannot find a reasonable match for her before she is of age she will soon find one for her self."

On the other hand, the Keyte proposal was not so attractive as it had at first appeared; the guardians had been looking into Sir William's affairs, and they had found that the estate was heavily encumbered with debts. The baronet owed, in fact, £10,000. He had sat for a number of years as Member of Parliament for Warwick, and heavy election expenses had reduced his fortune. If their ward were to marry young Thomas Keyte, the greater part of what she brought him would be swallowed up in settling those long-standing debts. Negotiations accordingly broke down in the spring of 1738; but Sir William, who was not to be easily shaken off, came to Town with a new offer early in the following year. Circumstances were now rather different. With every month that passed Charlotte Addison was becoming more and more difficult to control. She had carried her point about Aunt Combes, who had been down at Bilton again, keeping an open house for the young fellows of the neighbourhood, and even going so far as to give a ball for young Keyte on his birthday. Then apparently there had been a reaction; she had quarrelled with her niece and left Bilton, complaining to the Judge about Charlotte's bad temper, and declaring that she found it quite impossible to live with her. "Which all that know her is not so," wrote Sir John's sister charitably.

> Y^{e} worst of it is the amorous part at this time, and by all accounts she chouse to leave her rather than let it be seen that her management would not be alowed in town.

This was disturbing; and it was by no means the first hint that Sir John had received of his young cousin's growing inclination for the society of young men. The truth had, in fact, been set before him with startling frankness in a letter which his sister wrote from London on March 1, 1738:

> DEAR BROTHER,
>
> I give yu ye trouble of this letter by Mr. Dawney's earnest desire, because ye subject of it is more fit for a woman than a Gentleman to mention, especially as ye Person Concern'd is our relation, in short ye young Lady shows such great inclination to change her condition, that if ye Trustees do not make ye best terms for her they can with Mr. Kite, she will as soon as she is of age throw her self away on some very mean Person provided he has a pritty face. Sir Wm K. has been latly in town, & renew'd ye proposal to ye Trustees, & ye perticulors of ye Estate I have put on ye other side. Both Mr. D— and ye judge thinking ye Estate small, and ye debyt great, intended to put an end to ye affair, but ye latter Gentleman, haveing heard all over ye town that ye young Lady liked Mr. K—, came one morning to her & told her that tho they rejected ye match in point of fortune, yet if she would sincerely own her inclination, ye affair should go on. She beg'd a day or two to consider on it, and accordingly wrote him word that she desired not to Marry till she was of age, and might tell Mr. K— so, but if he

> saw Lady in that time he liked better than her self, she did not confine him. This declaration & a great many others too long to name, have plainly discover'd her intent is to keep Mr. K— in suspence, & when she is in her own liberty, either to throw her self away on a pritty fac'd fellow with nothing, or marry Mr. K— when she's so blown upon that she finds she can get no body else. She shows such inclination to have a great many danglers after her, that my Neice is almost ashamed to go wth her to any publick place, and her temper in relation to men is too Gross to mention, for my Neice says she has been with her but at one play, and never will go with her to another. She has had all ye advice from us relations (to wch she gives no answers) for to show her that ruin must ensue such behaviour, and at last ye result is that she has desired Mr. D. and ye judge to make ye best terms they can for her wth Mr. K. provided he may be admitted to visit her sooner than is allow'd by other familys. . . .

In fact, Mrs. Eyton was convinced that her brother would agree to the match now, as the only way to save their young cousin from ruin and disgrace. Besides, Charlotte had owned to liking young Keyte, and it was only her desire to have as many young men paying attention to her as possible that had kept her from declaring openly in his favour. Dismayed at those revelations, Sir John could only repeat his favourite remark: the girl ought to be married to a sober, discreet gentleman. He had always said so, and he said it again now.

About a week later his sister wrote again. Young Keyte had supplied some further particulars about his family affairs; the other two guardians had liked his frankness, and they were now inclined to settle the affair with as little delay as possible.

> His character is w^{ht} inclines ye Judg and Mr. D. to accept of it and ye more because ye Lady will not heare of its being put off but would have him admited as a lover without agreeing of settlements that she may have it in her power to drop him w^{hn}

> she sees any body better that she likes, so unknowne of her he is told not to send any more how-d-yee's nor hand her at any publick places at present till she com's to some resolution whither to go on or put him of. Both ye Trustees have don all they can to marry her but have had no offer so good as Mr. K.

Accordingly Mr. Dawnay informed young Keyte that his proposals were accepted, and Sir William immediately came to Town to see the affair settled; but the Judge was away on his circuit, and nothing could be finally decided until his return.

Early in May Sir John's niece, Mrs. Corbet, sent him a report of the way things were going. The formal arrangements were proceeding satisfactorily enough, but Mrs. Corbet was by no means easy in her mind about the young lady for whom those arrangements were being made. "I must now proceed to tell you," she wrote, with the icy intelligence of one female relative bringing her mind to bear upon another whom she disliked,

> that I doubt Miss A—'s temper will either give her self, or her Trustees, or both some further uneasiness, for I take her earnestness for this Match to proceed chiefly from her desire of marrying, she every day telling me that Mr. K—'s person is disagreeable to her & she cannot be happy but with a Man whom she thinks handsome & is in Love with. I have used all ye arguments to her I am Mistress of to persuade her rather to put it off now on ye foot of Settlements but she says her full determination is to let ye Match go on & if upon Mr. Keyt's visiting her at Bilton she cannot get rid of her aversion to his person she will then give him her final denyal.

Mrs. Corbet begged Sir John not to mention those facts to the Judge, fearing, no doubt, that he would put a stop to the match altogether if he found that Charlotte was not really fond of young Keyte. It would be much better, she felt, to let the affair proceed now, for this marriage was the girl's only hope. "And indeed," she concluded, "I have some thoughts that ye pleasure she will take in Courtship will reconcile her to his face." True love, as her father had once noted in one of his essays, "has ten thousand griefs, impatiences, and resentments, that render a man unamiable in the eyes of the person whose affection he solicits; besides that it sinks his figure, gives him fears, apprehensions, and poorness of spirit, and often makes him appear ridiculous where he has a mind to recommend himself." It may have been no worse than that with young Keyte.

What happened when the young man went to Bilton we do not know, for Sir John's letter book tells us nothing. Lady Broughton had stressed the importance of allowing two young people who were thinking of passing their lives together to be in the same house with each other for several days; and perhaps the days that young Keyte spent at Bilton were fatal to his chances. He seems to have been a worthy young fellow, but that was probably the last quality in him likely to appeal to Charlotte Addison, who was clearly looking for the sort of handsome beau that she had seen in the comedies of Farquhar or Cibber or Mrs. Centlivre. She had been surrounded by worthy people all her life, she was sprung from the loins of a particularly worthy and respected man, and nature is apt to rebel from too much moral excellence. But by failing to marry Thomas Keyte she had lost her second chance of becoming a baronet's lady, and it is unlikely that she ever got another.

And now, in 1740, death began to work great changes. Less than two months after her twenty-first birthday, Mr. Justice Denton, one of the best friends she ever had, whether she knew it or not, died at the age of sixty. He had done what he could to shape her life successfully, but he had been working all the time with indifferent clay. In the middle of the summer the Hon. John Dawnay followed him, freed at once from the suspense of waiting for a parent's death and from the insults and indignities to which his trusteeship had exposed him. But old Sir John Bridgeman, who had fully expected to go off before either of them, continued to look after his estate, to draft letters in his crabbed handwriting, and to explain to his correspondents that he was a very old man. He was, in fact, in his seventy-fourth year, and he lived on to within a few days of his eightieth birthday. Shortly after reaching her majority, Charlotte wrote him a letter of thanks for all the trouble he had taken as her guardian. For a young lady of twenty-one the handwriting is still remarkably childish, still, indeed, in the pothook stage, and the punctuation betrays a mind unable to sustain itself on any but the most timid flights. Charlotte's commas are not inserted with any real purpose ; they are not for the most part commas at all, but feeble pressures of the pen where she allowed it to rest before collecting her strength for the next brief effort of composition :

SIR,

I return you Thanks, for the favour of your Kind Letter, and am much obliged, to you, Sir, for your Care, of me, and my Affairs, During The Time of my Minority : and am Extreamly ashamed, to have been, so Long, in your Debt.

I hope that Tho I am now, Quite of Age, I may still Depend, upon your Friend-ship and Advice, and I beg, Sir, you will, be so good as to Concern your-self, with overlooking Bilton Estate, for me : I not being, at all used, to Such Sort, of Business, not that I would by any Means, have you, to take any Further Trouble then iust to See my Steward, now and Then, and to give him your Directions and in so Doing, I shall be very much beholden to you.

Who am with The utmost Esteem, Respect, and
Gratitude imaginable, Sir your most Obliged
Humble Servant,
CHA. ADDISON.

Sir John's reply was kind enough, but he was clearly unwilling to be bothered with her affairs any longer. In April of the following year the family lawyer sent him a formal release, and so that troublesome business was over at last. Later in that same year a queer thing happened. A fire broke out in Sir William Keyte's house at Norton in Gloucestershire, and the unfortunate baronet was burnt to death. Fires were all too frequent in the eighteenth century, but this was hardly an ordinary fire ; it was suggested in the newspapers that Sir William had started it himself, and that when his servants tried to drag him away from the blazing building he resisted them and preferred to perish in the flames. The newspapers, in fact, gave it out that he was lunatic, and perhaps he was. His efforts to restore the family fortunes through his son's marriage had failed, and despair at his mounting debts may have turned the baronet's wits. There was nothing left for his successor but to sell part of the estates, and this he did. He died, still unmarried, in 1755.

Charlotte, however, lived on. In the summer of 1741 she went to Scarborough for her health ; but after that her name appears no more in Sir John's letter book. She had still almost sixty years of life before her ; but with the death of Sir John she must have felt more and more solitary. There were still Bridgemans at Castle Bromwich, even though Sir John had passed away, and it appears that the ladies there were in the habit of visiting her ; but anything that one might write of those last sixty years would be only conjecture. Yet one can see Charlotte—now Miss Addison of Bilton, an ageing spinster —pacing about in the shade of the trees that her father had planted, skirting his fish-ponds in her walk, and no doubt throwing a few pieces of bread to the fat, unmolested chub, entertaining a few of the neighbouring ladies to tea perhaps, and pointing out to them her famous father's books and pictures, still kept just as he had left them.

As she grew older her infirmities increased. The deafness which had long troubled her became so bad that her domestics were forced to address her in respectful shouts. The oddity that had always marked her behaviour became more noticeable; it is from this final period, no doubt, that the legend of her mental derangement is derived. In her last years she was almost completely bed-ridden; but she used still to be carried in a chair to her father's favourite walk in the garden, "where she was placed for a time, for the benefit of the air, in a sheltered alcove, or mimic hermitage, a spot often dedicated by him to solitary thought." What thoughts passed through the mind of Charlotte Addison as she sat in her mimic hermitage we do not know. She had reached an age when it was no longer disgraceful not to think: perhaps she only sat there and stared at the fine trees that her father had planted. They were even older than herself, but not much.

She died at last in 1797. Even after she was dead, the memory of Addison's cultured presence survived for many years in his chairs and tables. "On entering the mansion," wrote a literary admirer of his in 1830, "a thrill of respect, even to veneration, unavoidably passes through the bosom of the examiner, when he finds that the furniture used by this learned man, still remains." But in the inventory which was drawn up on her death, the furniture had been dismissed rather contemptuously as "old." No one wanted Queen Anne chairs in 1797; they were merely out of date. And by 1797 no one wanted Charlotte Addison.

How casually and light-heartedly we bring new life

into the world! How rarely is there ever anything to justify our cheerfulness! What had Charlotte Addison done in all those eighty years of her existence; and what is to be said for such compact, unproductive, stationary ladies?

> Oh, better wrong and strife
> (By nature transient) than such torpid life.
> The silent Heavens have goings on,
> The stars have tasks, but these have none.

And yet Charlotte Addison had her place. For sixty years she had kept up her small establishment, she had employed a little labour. A handful of people at Bilton had earned a decent livelihood pruning her hedges, cleaning her silver, washing her dishes, grooming her horses, emptying out her earth-closets. It was not much, perhaps, but she had kept things going. Going for what? Ask the blackbird tugging his worm out of the lawn, or the toad squatting on a damp stone beneath the water tank. . . . Just going.

CURRENT INTELLIGENCE

1711–1712

This Day Monsieur de Guiscard, a French Papist, under Examination before a Committee of the Privy Council at the Cockpit, stabbed the Right Honourable Mr. Harley, Chancellor of the Exchequer, with a Penknife.

On Saturday in the Morning, the Marquis de Guiscard died in Newgate.

On Monday last, a Negroe Boy, about 14 Years old, of a good Complexion, indifferent Tall, speaks good English, with a Drugget Coat, Silk Waistcoat, with Red and Yellow Stripes, run away. Whoever gives notice to Nandoe's Coffee House . . .

Her Majesty has been pleased to create the Right Honourable Robert Harley a Peer of Great Britain.

On Saturday Morning, about 2 of the Clock, were seiz'd by three Messengers, and some of the Guards, in Drury Lane, the Effigies of the Pope, Devil, and Pretender, in a Box, with a Canopy over it, 4 Jesuits, 4 Cardinals, and 4 Fryars, and carried to the Rt. Hon. the Earl of Dartmouth's Office. They were designed to be carried in Procession that Evening, in order to be burnt at Night . . . to draw a great Mob together, who might have done a great deal of Mischief.

At the Queen's Theatre in the Haymarket, this present Tuesday, being the 4th of March, will be performed a new Opera called Hamlet.

An Entertainment by Mr. Clinch of Barnet, who imitates the Flute, Double Curtel, the Organ with 3 voices, the Horn, Huntsman and Pack of Hounds, the Sham-Doctor, the Old Woman, the Drunken Man, the Bells.

The most serene Elector Palatine being informed that the Ministers of his most Christian Majesty sent to the present Conferences for Peace, have therein made some Propositions. . . .

Are these Men met to put an End to a bloody War, to prevent the Ruin of Nations, the Burning of Cities, and the Destruction of People ? Do these Men act as if they design'd to stop the Bleeding of Europe, or to check the Crimson Deluge ? Merciful God !

All things being ready, we began to fire with our Howitzers, Mortars, and Cannon upon the Town ; and in six hours time we perceived that a Fire began in one of their Magazines.

Do these men know that the Sun has pass'd the Equator, and is advancing towards the Tropick ? . . . Do they consider that in one day an Action may happen, in which the Lives of 20 or 30 Thousand may be lost ? That on one Hour of Time which they throw away in foolish Forms, and dancing in the Circle of their Ridiculous Niceties, the Fate of Europe may depend ?

Her Majesty has been pleas'd to sign a Warrant for creating the Right Honourable Henry St. John, Esq. ; one of Her Majesty's Principal Secretaries of State, a Peer of Great Britain, by the title of Baron St. John, of Lidiard in the County of Wilts, and Viscount Bullingbrook.

Last week stood in the Pillory at Charing Cross and Temple Bar three Persons convicted at the Old Bailey for most horrid and impious Blasphemy, not fit to be repeated.

On Saturday Morning last, about 7 of the Clock, the Duke of Hamilton and the Lord Mohun fought a Duel in Hide-Park. The Lord Mohun died on the Spot; and my Lord Duke soon after he was brought home.

Incomparable Drops for the Palsie. . . . Sold only at Mrs. Cole's Toy-shop at the Dyal and Two Crowns against St. Dunstan's Church in Fleet-street, at 3s. 6d. a Bottle with Directions.

Just Publish'd; Popery Display'd . . .

Young Matthews

Ay, but to die, and go we know not where !

Measure for Measure

THE coming of the Hanoverians to England was one of those all too rare triumphs of common sense in history. England in 1714 decided to be happy under a prosaic King whom no one liked, rather than to risk a romantic unhappiness under the son of one who had made almost every one miserable. When Englishmen can persuade themselves to invite that contemptible thing, a foreigner, to rule over them, they are taking a step which only the most serious crisis would bring them even to contemplate.

Yet common sense has generally to make a hard fight for it, even in England. George I became King of Great Britain, not so much by the Grace of God, or by the goodwill of the people, as by the determination of the Whigs ; and for some years after he arrived in England he continued to be king only of the Whigs. Signs of dissatisfaction were obvious and frequent. There were riots and bonfires, Jacobite ballads on sale in the streets, seditious sermons in the churches, and ringing peals of disloyalty from the church steeples. "God damn King George ! " the Tories would shout as they came reeling out of some tavern, drunk but defiant. With all those manifestations of Jacobitism a singularly able Whig administration dealt patiently, and on the whole successfully. But progress was slow ; and there was nothing in George I, except the fact that he was not a Stuart, to make the Hanoverians popular, even with the Whigs.

Of all the dangers to public calm that the government had to contend with, the newspaper and the pamphlet, the political ballad and the lampoon, were perhaps the most serious and the most difficult to check. The government kept itself informed of what was happening in the printing trade by an extensive system of spies and informers; but in spite of its precautions and penalties a good deal of seditious printing was going on. Once the offending ballad or pamphlet had been printed off, it was easy enough for the enemies of the government to put it into circulation; the harm was done before the remedy could be applied.

Early in the month of June, 1719, copies of a paper called *Vox Populi, Vox Dei,* were being handed about unobtrusively in the streets of London. The contents of this apparently insignificant tract were sufficiently alarming to rouse the government to immediate action; for short as it was—no more than four pages—it was nothing less than a clear call to the people of England to cast off the Hanoverian King and restore the son of James II to the throne of his fathers. The exiled Prince was referred to as the Chevalier, and every one knew who was meant by that. Nor was there any ambiguity or timidity in the wording of *Vox Populi.* . . .

> The great opinion all courts have of this unfortunate prince's virtues shows he only wants to be known by us to be admired; and we only want the enjoyment of him to make us happy. . . . How long will you be ignorant of your strength? Count your numbers: sure you ought to fight with more resolution for liberty than your oppressors do for dominion. COUNT YOUR NUMBERS.

No government could afford to sit still and allow this sort of thing to pass unchallenged. About eight o'clock on the morning of June 7, less than four days after copies of *Vox Populi* had begun to appear on the streets, two of the King's messengers, John Hutchins and Thomas Roberts, entered the house of Mrs. Matthews, a printer in Pelican Court, Little Britain. There they arrested her son, John Matthews, who was still in bed. In his room they found several half sheets of the printed libel, including two which had clearly been marked for proof. Having duly secured those papers, they took their prisoner off to Newgate.

From the very first the case aroused the deepest interest. For one thing, Matthews was a handsome young fellow who conducted himself on all occasions with a kind of gallant effrontery. On being examined after his arrest, he met the grave warnings of his accusers by calmly taking snuff; and though often pressed to disclose the author of *Vox Populi*, he resolutely refused to do so. Clearly, too, he was a clever young man; for some of his questions during the early stages of his trial show that he was following very closely the evidence of the witnesses. But, what was still more in his favour, he was only eighteen years old, little more than a boy. It was indeed unfortunate for the government that it had to proceed against this handsome and high-spirited young fellow. At no time could it have counted on much popular support for the sort of prosecution it was now contemplating; but had the prisoner been a weak or shifty creature, like some of the witnesses who were later called at his trial, the case might have aroused less feeling.

The government, however, much as it might have preferred to make an example of some one less likely to awaken popular sympathy, was driven by the circumstances to prosecute this young printer. Young as he was, Matthews had already been in trouble more than once. In March of the previous year, he had been arrested for treasonable printing, only to make a sensational escape a few weeks later ; and he actually managed to remain at large until he was found one morning in July walking along the Strand, and taken off to prison again. The government had been lenient with him on this occasion, hoping that a severe warning would be enough to keep him out of trouble for the future ; but in this they misjudged their man badly. His elder brother, George Matthews, who took the precaution of having a padlock fixed on the press-room door in his mother's house, showed a better understanding of the young printer. Indeed, John Matthews had been taking advantage of his youth, and the fact that he had already been pardoned on that account only made him the bolder to offend.

Meanwhile the newspapers were seeing to it that the public did not forget about him. On July 18 it was reported that he had been examined by one of the Secretaries of State, and had proved " very refutary," and the following week, that he had been examined again. On September 4 the Grand Jury of Middlesex found a bill of High Treason against him ; he was committed to Newgate, and loaded with irons. Mrs. Powell's weekly journal, *The Orphan Reviv'd,* noted on this occasion the " undaunted and resolute temper " with which he bore up under his troubles. Two weeks later he made an attempt to escape from Newgate. " Last Wednesday Night," we read in Applebee's *Weekly Journal,* " young Matthews, the Printer, had found a Design to escape out of Newgate, having alter'd the Colour of his Eyebrows and Face ; but the Matter being discover'd to the Keepers, they prevented it." On October 27 a scandalised busy-body wrote to the Secretary's office to inform him of the outrageous behaviour of the young printer in Newgate Chapel. This tell-tale had not attended the Chapel service himself; he had the story at second hand from a friend of his who had occupied the same pew as Matthews. Not only did Matthews and a fellow-prisoner talk and laugh during the service, but Matthews

> took a paper out of his pocket and both did read it in one of their hats, which paper two young women in the seat with signs of indignation told my friend afterwards was a ballad. My friend further tells me that Matthews standing up and leaning over the pew beckoned to one of the Prison Officers, saying damme why do you not bring the wine? Soon after it appeared the wine was brought, both went out of the pew into a by-place, and as he was informed, drank it, and so came in.

On the morning of October 31, after a delay of several days due to a legal point raised by his counsel, the trial of John Matthews began at the Old Bailey. The Attorney-General appeared for the Crown, and Matthews was defended by Mr. Hungerford and Mr. Ketelby, two of the ablest counsel of the day. He began by taking exception to thirty-five jurymen, but this spirited gesture only served to delay the opening of proceedings a little longer. Some idea of the excitement in Court may be gathered from the fact that before the first witness was called the foreman of the jury had to ask that the Court might be kept quiet, or it would be impossible for them to hear the evidence.

The Attorney-General then opened for the Crown. On the whole he stated the case against Matthews very fairly, without either exaggeration or vindictiveness.

"I am sorry," he told the jury,

> for anyone that falls under such an accusation, but more especially for one so young; but, gentlemen, compassion is neither your business nor mine; that belongs to another place, as the case shall appear.

The Crown case was based on an Act of VI Anne, which declared that any person who should "maliciously, advisedly, and directly, by writing or printing, maintain and affirm, that our sovereign lady the queen that now is, is not the lawful and rightful queen of these realms, or that the pretended prince of Wales, who now stiles himself king of Great Britain, or king of England, by the name of James the 3rd, or king of Scotland, by the name of James the 8th, hath any right or title to the crown of these realms . . ." should be adjudged guilty of high treason.

The Crown then called the first witness, John Hutchins, one of the two messengers who had arrested Matthews on July 7, and Hutchins at once plunged into that sort of recitation which bears only too obvious traces of having been carefully memorised.

> I brought him to Newgate. When I came for him, I suppose, says he, I am going to Newgate, and that a bill of high-treason will be found against me? Yes, says I, that there is already. I advised him to tell the author, and it would be the better for him. He said, I know I shall be hanged; but I have nothing to do, but let the money fly to get a good jury, that is all: He said those that set him to work were a pack of dogs, good for nothing but over a bottle of wine, or a pot of beer.

Hutchins was going on to explain that he found some copies of *Vox Populi* in the prisoner's pocket and others scattered about the room when a question from Matthews forced him to admit that actually he had not found anything—it was the other messenger who had done the searching: Hutchins himself had merely guarded the door. "I desire to know," was the prisoner's next request, "if all these papers were taken in this room." Hutchins was shaping badly; he had to admit now that several were found in a box in another room,—"but he said it was his room and his box." Later, however, the defence was able to elicit the important information that it was William Harper, one of the chief witnesses for the Crown, who slept in this room—an inner room opening off the one occupied by Matthews. Hutchins had carefully marked the papers ("This taken out of his pocket by me and Roberts"); but under cross-examination he had to admit that the marking did not take place in the prisoner's room, but about two hours later, after he had seen his prisoner safely lodged in Newgate. The evidence of Roberts, the other messenger, agreed on the whole with that of Hutchins.

The next witness was William Harper, a young apprentice of Mrs. Matthews. About four o'clock on the morning of June 3 Matthews had called him up, and said that he had a job for him. The job turned out to be the printing of *Vox Populi*. Harper went into the press-room and helped Lawrence Vezey to work off an impression of a thousand copies; he saw Matthews compose part of it from the manuscript, and in Court he was able to identify the type used.

He was succeeded in the witness box by Lawrence Vezey, a thoroughly disagreeable old man, determined to save his own skin, at whatever cost to the prisoner.

On Wednesday the 3rd of June last, I went to work, as usual, in the morning, between four and five o'clock. When I came into the court, the apprentice lies backward, I called out, William! The apprentice opened his window up two-pair-of-stairs; says he, Old gentleman, the door is open. I went up into the press-room. Mr. John Matthews came up; says

> he, Old gentleman, I have a job for you to do. Says I, Is the work in haste? Yes, it must be done soon. Then came up William Harper; I asked him what it was. Says he, I don't know, he hath got a job to do. About nine o'clock I went to market, when my companion went to breakfast; in the mean time, there was a form composed in quarto, called *Vox Populi, Vox Dei*, I cannot say who composed it; then John Matthews was gone out of the room. When I came back from market, and my companion had breakfasted, I went to work again, as usual; and Mr. John Matthews came up, and said, Damn it, I have transposed the pages; I saw no proof sheet; but he takes out the form, and lays it on the press, and puts it into order.

The prisoner's counsel immediately proceeded to cross-examine the old printer, but there was little hope of shaking his evidence. He addressed both counsel obsequiously as "My Lord," but stuck to his story.

Two master printers were next called by the Crown to explain to the jury the mystery of printing, and to make clear the significance of the proof sheets found in Matthews' room. They were followed by Mr. Delafaye, an under-secretary, who testified that when examined by the Lords Justices Matthews had admitted to owning the papers found in his room.

The Crown having called all their witnesses, Mr. Hungerford rose on behalf of Matthews to submit that there was no case to answer. It was clearly impossible to persuade the jury that Matthews was not involved in the printing of *Vox Populi*, and the defence therefore tried to show that he was being prosecuted under an act which no longer applied to such a case as his. "We all know," Mr. Hungerford argued, "that the matter under the consideration of the parliament at that time was, that since upon the Queen's death, the next succession was like to be beyond sea, to secure that the

Protestant succession should take place (as now, God be praised, to all our comforts, it hath)." Queen Anne, in fact, was dead, and George I seated securely on her throne; the act was practically obsolete, and should not now be revived against the unfortunate prisoner. Nor had the Crown succeeded in proving malice: the boy was merely rash. "Malice and design are commonly the temper of advanced years, and not of apprentice boys." Mr. Hungerford then proceeded to pour scorn on the evidence of Hutchins and Roberts. "Each of them," he remarked sarcastically, "contends for the honour of picking the boy's pocket." As for the evidence of his being concerned in printing the libel:

> Printing itself is but a mechanical art, and one may print a whole volume, and not know one jot of the contents, drift, and tendency of the book; and in the present case the prisoner is not the master-printer; he is but an apprentice, and the trade is carried on by his mother, and elder brother.

Mr. Hungerford was succeeded by Mr. Ketelby, who criticised the Crown case as being based on nothing but innuendoes. The unfortunate youth was entitled to the benefit of every doubt. The boy . . . the unfortunate youth: this was undoubtedly the safest line for the defence to take, and Mr. Ketelby concluded adroitly enough by knocking another year off the reckoning. "A boy," he told the jury, "of seventeen. . . ."

At this point the ultimate verdict was still, perhaps, uncertain; the tide only turned against Matthews when the defence called his own brother. The trial had now lasted many hours. The October daylight was fading out of the Court; Mr. Hungerford had already been forced to complain that the light was so bad he could not see to quote from a document. George Matthews stepped into the witness box obviously intending to help

Mr. John Matthews, the Printer,

His laſt Farewel to the WORLD.

NO ſtoney heart can ceaſe to ſhed a tear,
To ſee a youth cropt in his blooming [years;
Having ſo little time for to repent
Before he to another World is ſent.

I poor *John Matthews* muſt reſign and die,
A wretched Death upon the gallows high,
I little thought when I this thing did do,
The fatal accidence that would enſue.

But now before that I this world depart,
I freely do forgive withal my heart,
Thoſe that did ſwear my tender life away,
And likewiſe thoſe who did me firſt betray.

When at the bar I was arraign'd and caſt,
This cruel ſentence was upon me paſt;
John Matthews for *high Treaſon* you muſt die,
Firſt to be hang'd upon the gallows high,

While you're alive thy body be cut down,
Thy bowels in the burning fire thrown,
And then thy limbs for to be cut in twain,
At which I bow'd and thank'd them for the ſame.

Alas, alas, my tender mother dear,
Till monday laſt this news ſhe did not hear;
And when ſhe came indeed to know the ſame
Like one diſtracted ſhe unto me came.

To ſee her tears it made my heart to bleed,
'Tis ten times worſe than death it ſelf indeed;
My Child, my Child was all her aged cry;
I little thought that you this Death would die.

But all her tears will not avail I ſee,
No, no reprieve nor mercy there's for me;
My tender years will yield me no relief,
O die I muſt, unto my friends 'tis grief.

Some ſay my Brother took my life away,
'Twas innocently ſpoke what he did ſay;
So none afflict my friends or parents dear,
They all of me have took a ſpecial care.

I did not think indeed to dye ſo ſoon,
My morning Sun, alas! goes down at noon;
My time is ſhort, is ſhort, is ſhort indeed,
But I'll to heaven for Mercy call with ſpeed.

But now before this World I do forſake,
Let all young youth a warning by me take;
For Earth affords no hope nor truſt at all,
If you for mercy ſhould have cauſe to call.

O Lord, who dwells above in Heaven high,
In Mercy Chriſt give ear unto my cry,
And tho' my Body it is cut in twain,
Receive my Soul in Glory there to reign.

London: Printed in the Year, 1719.

A BROADSHEET BALLAD ON THE DEATH OF MATTHEWS

his brother, and, if necessary, to suppress a good deal that he knew; but under a ruthless cross-examination from the Attorney-General he ultimately broke down, and practically gave away his brother's case. "As to the calling of George Matthews for a witness," said one of the Crown counsel later, "if I had been a friend to the prisoner, I should have reckoned myself very unhappy in so doing." It was indeed a tragic error, and one can only suspect that George Matthews had concealed from his brother's counsel the extent to which he was implicated in the case himself. The trouble began when the Attorney-General suddenly passed him a letter, and asked whether he recognised the signature. Did he believe it to be in his brother's handwriting? Matthews at first replied that he could not be certain. The question was repeated.

Matthews: I cannot say directly as to believing it, but I cannot swear to it.

Att.-Gen.: Have you never seen him write?

Matthews: I cannot say but I have.

Att.-Gen.: You have frequently seen him write. I ask you (mine is a direct question), do you, or do you not, believe the name, John Matthews, to be your brother's handwriting, upon the oath you have taken?

Matthews repeats several times that he cannot be positive.

Att.-Gen.: Why do you trifle with the Court? Cannot you say, whether you believe it, or not believe it?

Matthews: I say, if you please to give me leave to introduce what I have to say, I believe it is something like it.

But this, of course, is not good enough for the Attorney-General. He presses for a plain "yes" or "no," and Matthews begins to weaken. At last he admits, "I have some reason to believe it."

> Att.-Gen.: Do not let me mistake you, I think you say you do believe it? Do you believe it is not your brother's handwriting?
>
> Matthews: Give me leave, let me state the question; what you ask me is, whether I believe it is my brother's handwriting? I do believe it.

The Attorney-General has now gained his point. But what, in fact, is the point? For that the crowded Court has still to wait a little longer. Meanwhile George Matthews flounders on, trying to put the best complexion upon his evidence, but only, of course, making matters worse. "If I might have the liberty of telling the connexion of circumstances," he begs pathetically on one occasion, realising, no doubt, where the Attorney-General's cross-examination is leading. Had he stuck to his original intention not to identify his brother's signature he would probably have got himself into serious trouble, but he might have prevented the Crown from using a piece of highly incriminating evidence. The letter, he now explains, is in his own handwriting; he wrote it out for his brother to sign. He took it to Newgate in the evening and pushed it through the grating. Seven or eight minutes later, the letter was returned to him, again through the grating, signed by his brother. He took it to the office of Mr. Secretary Craggs, but some one told him that Mr. Craggs had gone to dine with my Lord St. John at Battersea; so he hurried out to Battersea. Mr. Craggs was still at dinner when he arrived, but some time later he came out and spoke to

Matthews in the garden. . . . "I told him, Sir, I had gotten a paper from my brother."

The Attorney-General now asks that the letter be read in Court; but to this the prisoner's counsel immediately objects on the ground that the signature has not really been proved. The Lord Chief Justice argues the point, and finally Judge Tracey, recollecting, perhaps, that judges, no less than jurymen must dine, exclaims, "We must have never an end of things, at this rate." The Lord Chief Justice decides at length that the letter may be read, and the curiosity of the Court is satisfied. It is a statement, purporting to come from John Matthews himself, that he is heartily sorry for the crimes he has committed against his most sacred Majesty, King George, and that the manuscript of *Vox Populi* was given him by one, John Broderick, living in Shire Lane. This signed confession must have come as a severe shock to the defence; but Mr. Hungerford rises gallantly and assures the Court that he is not sorry this paper has come to light. . . . "Here is a witness bound to do service to a brother in prison. Moved with compassion, he forms a paper of this nature, not by any instructions from the prisoner at the bar."

But the letter was, no doubt, the finishing touch with a weary jury. John Matthews had signed that statement; you couldn't get away from that. Now came the speeches of counsel, and finally the Lord Chief Justice's summing up. The jury retired to consider their verdict, and after a short absence returned. They found the prisoner guilty.

But if they thought they were now free to go home they were mistaken. The defence was not nearly beaten yet. Mr. Hungerford rose and moved for an arrest of judgment. In the indictment the word "impressit" had been used to signify "printed." But this Latin verb had several other meanings; it might, for example, mean "stamped." There followed a long argument on this point while the unhappy prisoner stood in the dock awaiting his sentence. Mr. Serjeant Cheshire pointed out for the Crown that it was just as true to say that the Latin word "liber" meant several different things—"a book," "Bacchus," "free," "the bark of a tree"—and yet no one would think of mixing up those various meanings. To this Mr. Hungerford very learnedly retorted that bark was used for writing upon before either vellum or paper was in use, and that "liber" meaning "free" was an adjective. . . . "As for 'liber' signifying 'Bacchus,' the serjeant hath been at dinner, he hath eat and drank plentifully, I dined with him, and I find he hath forgot part of the name of Bacchus, for he is called 'Liber Pater,' and not 'liber' only, that I remember." To one not familiar with the conduct of justice in the eighteenth century the whole of this learned discussion might seem only a futile way of delaying the sentence a little longer; yet prisoners frequently escaped punishment through just such a flaw in the indictment as the defence were now seeking to prove. On this occasion, however, the judges were of opinion that the indictment was worded without any ambiguity.

Mr. Hungerford now made one last desperate attempt, and brought forward another objection founded on the wording of the Act of Parliament on which the charge had been made; but this, too, was set aside. Not far short of midnight, the Lord Chief Justice proceeded to pass the sentence reserved for those guilty of high treason. Young Matthews was sentenced to be drawn on a hurdle to the place of execution, and there hanged by the neck; while he was still alive, he was to be cut down, the bowels taken out of his belly, and burnt before his eyes ; his head was to be cut off, and his body divided into four quarters, to be disposed of as His Majesty might think fit. And finally, as if in acknowledgment of the fact that King George's authority over his subjects did not extend beyond their bodies—"May God have mercy on your soul." To which Matthews ironically replied : "I thank you, my Lord, a very easy sentence."

John Matthews had now only four days left to live. On Sunday, when his condemnation sermon was preached at Newgate, the chapel was crowded to the doors. To some of that congregation the young man was a popular hero, to others, perhaps, a dangerous traitor ; but to every one in Newgate Chapel on that Sunday morning he was the most important young man in London.

The day of his execution was exceedingly wet, but huge crowds had gathered all along the road to Tyburn to see him go by. A woman who had a house at Tyburn took more than £10 from spectators who were willing to pay her for the privilege of looking on at the execution in comfort from her windows. If they went there hoping to see the young printer's bowels taken out and burnt, they were disappointed, for that part of the sentence was remitted ; but they were rewarded by seeing him bleed from his nose and mouth as he swung on the rope. He did not gratify the crowd with a speech, nor did he make merry with his last few minutes on earth ; he did, however, die with composure, and showed no signs of terror. On the whole, it must have been reckoned a satisfactory afternoon, in spite of the wretched weather. It was a show that you could never see at the play-house ; a procession with movement and incident and the red-coats of the soldiers for colour, the dead cart slowly coming along in a noisy cloud of murmuring and cheering, the long pause beneath the gallows tree while the hangman made his final arrangements, and at the last the young printer swinging in the rain.

For young Matthews the drama was now over ; but though the chief actor had played out his part, there were others for whom the play was not yet finished. It was a long time before his brother's conduct was forgotten. George Matthews found himself blamed on all sides for the part he had played in the trial, and before it ; he was forced to justify himself by inserting advertisements in the newspapers, and by publishing a short vindication of his conduct, which was given away gratis to anyone who cared to ask for it.

The usual ballads and " last dying words " appeared on the streets immediately after the execution, dwelling with gloomy relish on all the more poignant circumstances of the case :

> I poor John Matthews must resign and die,
> A wretched Death upon the gallows high,
> I little thought when I this thing did do,
> The fatal accidence that would ensue. . . .
>
> Alas, alas, my tender mother dear,
> Till monday last this news she did not hear ;
> And when she came indeed to know the same
> Like one distracted she unto me came.
>
> To see her tears it made my heart to bleed,
> 'Tis ten times worse than death it self indeed ;
> My Child, my Child, was all her aged cry ;
> I little thought that you this Death would die.

This is wretched enough, but it is not quite so blatant as the verses of another ballad writer, who calls upon his Muse to mourn :

My Muse replies, what is his death to me,
Since Justice sent him to hang on a Tree,
His Bowels burnt while he alive should be,
His Head and Quarters at the King's Disposal,
Which we may well suppose to be as usual. . . .

It is, however, in the fate of Harper and Vezey that the most interesting echoes of the case are to be found. The Government had secured the conviction of Matthews by frightening those two printers into giving the evidence that ultimately hanged him. Without those two there could have been no conviction. For some time after the trial, Harper and Vezey remained in custody, not so much as a punishment for having been concerned in seditious printing as for their own protection. The printers as a class were far from being uniformly loyal to King George, but they were singularly loyal to the members of their own trade, and an informer knew that he might expect rough treatment from his fellows. On December 4, Harper, still in confinement, wrote to Delafaye, begging that he might not be forgotten:

Worthy Sir,

I am desir'd by Mr. Vezey to write to your Worship, for he is very much troubled with an Asthma, and Confinement is very detremental to him: Therefore he humbley hopes that your worship would Discharge him that he may go into the Countrey for a little air. I hope your worsp. will pardon me for troubling your worship as I have done, but I know Persons of your Worship's Vertue and Goodness are redier to grant Favours to the unfortunate than they are to ask. I return your worship abundance of thanks for your Inestimable promise to me, which has laid an Injunction upon me to pray for your Worship as long as I live. I hope your Worship will Discharge us as Soon as possible, for my long Confinement has much Impair'd my Health, and I want Several necessaries since these wicked people has sett my friends against me, So that I hope your Worship will not take it Ill, and your worship will for ever oblige your worship's most obedient Vasels

to command
W. Harper
L. Vezy.

The " inestimable promise " mentioned by Harper refers to an assurance given to him that he would be compensated for the loss of his employment ; the Government had made use of the two printers and were now morally bound to provide for them. But the days dragged by, and nothing happened : there were matters of more pressing importance to be attended to than the immediate future of two informers who had now exhausted their usefulness. On the 16th Harper wrote again to Delafaye, asking for money ; and on the 28th to Secretary Craggs himself, begging for some compensation for the loss of his friends and his employment, and praying that he might be discharged without longer delay. . . . " Since the tryal and execution of Matthews I have not had a friend come to bring me any thing." Seven months later, on July 20, 1720, he was formally petitioning the Treasury for some relief. In the interval he had tried to carry on his trade of printing, but it was no good : people kept insulting him or threatening him, and no one would give him any job to do because he had informed against Matthews. From a letter of October 12, however, it seems probable that he was eventually provided for by some grant from the exchequer, for he writes on that date of investing money received in a printing-press, and asks for the privilege of doing all the printing required at the Customs House.

It is not impossible that Harper managed to re-establish himself in time ; but on old Vezey the resentment of the public told more heavily. On the January following the execution of Matthews, the Society of Journeyman Printers deprived him of his membership. The reason they gave for their decision must have annoyed the Government: Vezey was expelled for "treasonable printing." There can be only one interpretation of this unwonted burst of loyalty on the part of the printers; Vezey was being expelled, not because he had helped to print *Vox Populi*, but because he had not held his tongue about it. The treason, in fact, was to his own profession, not to King George; the journeyman printers were expressing their contempt for the Government and its tool in a way which made any reply impossible. There was nothing left for Vezey to do now but to go home and die in his bed. So, in fact, he did. Five months later the miserable old man was dead; it remained only to put him in the ground.

On the night of June 22, 1720, he was carried in his coffin to the churchyard at Islington, where a grave had been dug for him. It was a chance not to be missed. The journeyman printers had already shown what they thought of the old man; it was now the turn of the apprentices. As the coffin was borne along towards the graveyard, it became obvious that some mischief was afoot. A crowd, mostly composed of young men in the printing trade who had walked out from London for the occasion, had gathered in the graveyard, to see that Vezey got the sort of funeral that they thought he deserved. The printers were joined by the usual loafers and bystanders, and before long the crowd was well on its way to becoming a riotous mob. The bearers were forced to set down the coffin, and the mob, making a rush to Vezey's open grave, amused themselves by filling it, as one contemporary account puts it, with "nastiness," and with "causing a great tumult." There could be no burying that night; old Vezey was carried back along the road he had come. But the next day he had his revenge. A number of the rioters were arrested, including Michael Matthews, another brother of the young printer's, and order was re-established at Islington. And then came the final triumph. The Government was taking no more chances; the sooner the old man was under the ground the better it would be for every one concerned. That night a detachment of the Foot-guards marched out to Islington from Whitehall, "to see the corpse bury'd, and preserve the peace," and at last the earth was allowed to close quietly over his grave. And so Lawrence Vezey passed out of the news, with the soldiers standing by in their scarlet uniforms preserving the peace, and enfolding him in the warmth of their own importance. The old man had made a good end, a better end than his wizened little soul deserved.

CURRENT INTELLIGENCE

1713-1714

PAX, PAX, PAX, Or A PACIFICK POSTSCRIPT to the POST-BOY. London, April 3, 1713. An Express of the Signing of the Peace. This day, about Twelve of the Clock arrived here the Hon. George St. John, Esq.; Brother to the Right Hon. Lord Viscount Bolingbroke, Express from Utrecht with the Joyful News, That on Tuesday last the Peace was signed by the Plenipotentiaries of the Queen of Great Britain, the King of France, the States of Holland, the Duke of Savoy, the King of Prussia, and the King of Portugal. . . .

Canterbury, May 13. This being the Day for Proclaiming the Peace in this City, early in the Morning the Streets and Houses were all drest with Greens, and nigh 100 Garlands hung cross them very richly furnished with Plate to a great Value; Carpets and Pictures adorn'd the Houses; the Bells at the Cathedral-Church, and all the other Parish Churches, rang almost all Day.

A Tryall of Skill to be fought at the Bear Garden in Marrow-Bone-Fields, at the Boarded House, near Tyburn-Road, on Wednesday next, being the 27th of May, beginning precisely at 2 a Clock, between Timothy Gorman, Serjeant, Master of the Noble Science of Self Defence, and John Parkes of Coventry, Master of the said Science.

Abundance of rich Masquerade Cloths are making against Thursday next, when his Excellency the Duke d'Aumont will give another splendid Entertainment to many of the Nobility and Gentry.

. . . Her Majesty came to Hampton-Court about 3 *of the Clock in the Afternoon; and yesterday, at the same Hour, to her Royal Palace at St. James's, in perfect Health, to the great Satisfaction of all her Loyal Subjects; and the Evening concluded with Ringing of Bells, Bonfires, Illuminations, and other Demonstrations of Joy suitable to so happy an Occasion.*

The Right Hon. the Earl of Oxford is out of the Place of Lord High Treasurer; the same will be put in Commission.

The Duke of Shrewsbury is made Lord High Treasurer of Great-Britain, in the Room of the Earl of Oxford.

London, Aug. 1. *This day, at half an Hour past Seven in the Morning, died our late most Gracious Sovereign* QUEEN ANNE, *in the fiftieth Year of her Age, and the Thirteenth of her Reign; a Princess of exemplary Piety and Virtue. Her Majesty complain'd on Thursday last of a Pain in her Head; The next Day she was seized with Convulsion Fits, and for some time lost the Use of her Speech and Senses, which, tho' She afterwards recovered upon the Application of proper Remedies, She continued in a very weak and languishing Condition till she expired. Upon her Death the Lords of the Privy Council immediately assembled at St. James's, and gave Orders for Proclaiming the Most High and Mighty Prince George, Elector of Brunswick-Lunenburg, King of Great Britain, France, and Ireland. . . .*

Yesterday came Advice of the Arrival of the Duke and Dutchess of Marlborough at Dover.

Joseph Addison Esq.; Member for Malmesbury, is appointed Secretary to the Lords Justices.

London, Aug. 7. *We patiently expect the safe Arrival of the King. . . .*

London, Aug. 10. *N.B. In our last, in the London Article, for patiently, read impatiently.*

Last Night the Queen's Bowels were deposited in King Henry the Seventh's Chapel in Westminster Abbey.

Last Night the Corpse of Her late Majesty Queen Anne was interred with due Solemnity in Westminster Abbey.

On Saturday Night last, between Six and Seven in the Evening, His Majesty landed at Greenwich, from whence he proceeded Yesterday towards Noon, to make his Royal Entry into this City.

Yesterday the King and the Prince passed through the City to St. James's. The Procession was magnificent, the Balconies, Windows, and Scaffolds adorned with Tapistry etc. The Crowd was exceeding great, the Acclamations loud, and the Joy universal.

The Funeral of John, Duke of Marlborough

In that day shall there be a great mourning in Jerusalem, as the mourning of Hadadrimmon in the valley of Megiddon.

Zechariah xii, 11

At four o'clock on the morning of Saturday, June 16, 1722, there expired at Windsor an old gentleman who had been ailing for several years. With careful tending he had entered upon his seventy-third year; but from the day that he had been struck down, six years ago, with a paralytic stroke, he had been something of a trouble to himself and his friends, a sad ruin of a man sitting in melancholy grandeur amongst the impressive relics of a great career. For this old gentleman was no ordinary person, but the most high mighty, and most noble prince, John Churchill, Duke and Earl of Marlborough, Marquess of Blandford, Lord Churchill of Sandbridge in the County of Hereford, Baron of Aymouth in the County of Berwick in Scotland, Prince of the Most Holy Roman Empire, Captain-General of His Majesty's forces, Master-General of the Ordnance, one of the Lords of His Majesty's most honourable Privy Council, and Knight of the Most Noble Order of the Garter. For one who had begun life as plain John Churchill, his was a remarkable achievement; and it was almost all due to his own efforts and those of his remarkable wife, aided, no doubt, as his enemies were never tired of suggesting, by the frailty of a sister, upon whom James II had cast his not too discriminating eye.

If great generals could contrive to die when their fame was at its height, and preferably with sword in hand at the head of their armies, their end would be memorable indeed; but ordinarily they come home and die in bed of coughs and palsies, and their passing seems curiously irrelevant.

> To have done is to hang
> Quite out of fashion, like a rusty mail,
> In monumental mockery—

and in time of peace, too, the soldier's virtues are apt to appear unattractive, the soldier himself rather a bore, and his claim to the public's gratitude excessive. It was so with Marlborough, but only to a limited extent. For one thing he had been a quite remarkably successful general: even his enemies, who sometimes charged him with cowardice and corruption, and who pointed out that one or two of his victories were among the bloodiest on record, were forced to admit that he did go on winning battles and storming towns and raising sieges with unfailing resource, and that his soldiers were ready to die for him whenever he gave the word. It was no good pretending that Marlborough's victories were all due to luck, or to the bravery of his troops, or to the cowardice and corruption of his military opponents. After you had said your worst about his conduct and character, and had done your best to explain away his successes in the field, the majority of your listeners would still be quite convinced that he was a very great general. When Marlborough died in 1722, therefore, more than ten years after his last campaign, his countrymen realised that they had lost in him, not just another eminent general, but one of the greatest soldiers in the world's history.

But there was another good reason why Marlborough's death should be a great public event; he had become a cause, a political issue. The Tories who had been so anxious in 1712 to bring a long and expensive war to an end, had gone about it by first of all getting rid of Marlborough; they had brought to light certain irregularities in his handling of public money, and in this way secured his dismissal from the command of the English forces. A speedy peace was what the Tories were looking for, and now it was more than ever necessary to them; for if after Marlborough's dismissal the French had begun to recover their lost ground, there might easily have been a public outcry to recall him. Soon afterwards, therefore, the Tories proceeded to make a peace with the French which, in the eyes of the Whigs, simply threw away the fruits of victory. Whatever may be said in favour of the Peace of Utrecht, it certainly brought to an end Marlborough's career as a soldier; and for that, and for his disgrace in 1712, he had to thank the Tories. And so, little as some of them might care for Marlborough, the Whigs were driven from mere opposition to be his champions; and for the rest of his life he lived on in princely retirement as a Whig hero, the man that the unpatriotic Tories had treated with such ingratitude. The more he could be made to look a hero, the more disgraceful appeared the conduct of the Tories, and the more patriotic that of the Whigs, who had supported him in his glorious if bloody, campaigns.

Such was the position when the broken old soldier breathed his last in the summer of 1722; and as soon as news of his death reached London it became evident to the Whigs that something really unprecedented was called for, a national funeral on so magnificent a scale that the Tories might see once and for all how great was the man they had tried to dishonour. And whether the Whigs roused themselves to action or not, Sarah, Duchess of Marlborough, had no intention of letting the occasion pass without a splendid tribute to her lord; she would give him such a funeral as would make the death of kings look trivial in comparison, and would make "her neighbour George" over at St. James's realise the almost royal greatness of the dead hero.

It was an age of pompous and elaborate obsequies. Death was a social event of great dignity; and the dead, lying in state amidst wax candles burning night and day in their silver sconces, and attended by the professional grief of paid mourners, contributed very considerably to the employment of the living. A nation which has learnt to bury its dead with sufficient ostentation has gone a long way towards solving the problem of unemployment. In the eighteenth century the relatives of the deceased had to meet a heavy bill of expenses. Not only had they to pay the wax-chandler and the hired mourners, but they had to cope with such separate items as gloves, mourning rings, hatbands of crape, the coffin, the woollen shroud, torches and tapers, claret for the mourners, printed cards of invitation, and, if the dead person were of sufficient rank, escutcheons for the hearse, and the cost of embalming his corpse. Velvet palls, mourning cloaks, plumes, and hangings of sable for the rooms could be hired, but they were often very costly. Over all this expenditure the undertakers, or, as they were usually called, the upholders, presided with conscious importance. Gay describes an upholder waiting impatiently in the street for the death of his client,

> As vultures o'er a camp, with hovering flight,
> Snuff up the future carnage of the fight—

and they were frequently satirised by the dramatists and the essayists. But they could afford to smile, for they had succeeded in imposing a competitive spirit in public mourning which led to greater and greater extravagance in the burial of the dead. A system which provided employment for so many different tradesmen, from the haberdasher to the vintner, and the coach-hirer to the chandler, and so impressive a spectacle to the general public, could not easily be allowed to decay; it was in the interest of almost everyone to maintain it, and if the proper disposal of the dead often led to the impoverishment of their survivors, public opinion was too strong to permit of any economy in the last rites. Nor were costly funerals confined to the nobility or to those wealthy citizens whose wives could afford to pay for such pageantry; the black feathers of elaborate grief waved and nodded in the processions of the poor. In dedicating one of her comedies to "The Magnificent Company of Upholders," Mrs. Centlivre pays a satirical tribute to their importance in the life of her time:

> All Ranks and Conditions are obliged to you; the Aged and the Young, the Generous and the Miser, the well-descended and the baser born. The Escutcheons garnish out the Hearse, the Streamers and Wax Lights let us into the Name of a Man, which all his Life had been hid in Obscurity; and many a Right Honourable would fall unlamented, were it not for your decent Cloaks and dismal Faces, that look as sorrowfully as the Creditors they leave unpaid. What an immense Sum might be rais'd from your Art to carry on the War, would you, like true Britons, exert your Power! The People being fond of sights, what might not be gather'd at a Funeral, when the Rooms are clad in Sable, the Body dress'd out with all your skilful Care, the Tapers burning in their Silver Sockets, the weeping Virgins fixt like Statues round, and aromatic Gums perfume the Chambers. I think it preferable to the Puppet-show, and a Penny a Head for all the Curious would, I dare be positive, amount to more than the Candle-Tax.

AN EIGHTEENTH CENTURY FUNERAL INVITATION

There was every reason, therefore, why the funeral of Marlborough should provide a spectacle of quite unusual magnificence. Custom demanded it; the public from being long glutted with funeral pomps of noble proportion had come to expect it; and the Duke himself deserved it.

He was hardly cold before rumour was busy with his funeral. The newspapers kept their readers well informed about the latest developments. "We hear," said the *Daily Journal,* "that in about a Fortnight or three Weeks' time the Funeral of his Grace the Duke of Marlborough will be perform'd in a most Noble, Magnificent and Publick Manner." Meanwhile twenty-four great families had gone into mourning, for the Duke was connected through the marriage of his four daughters to the Dukes of Montagu and of Bridgwater, and to the Earls of Sunderland and of Godolphin, with a considerable part of the nobility of England. The weekly journals were printing obituary notices of unusual length; and from time to time they favoured their readers with elegies on the dead Duke:

> Marlb'rough's Soul has ta'en its Flight:
> Who shall now our Battles fight?

—one can at least detect the tone of honest admiration; the bard is doing his best.

As the days passed, more intimate details about the approaching funeral were given to the public. The body was to lie in state for fifteen days at Marlborough House, and the necessary apparatus was being prepared for it. It was said that a sum of £30,000 was going to be spent on the ceremony. A fine open hearse was being built by Awberry, the King's coachman; the Company of Upholders had provided themselves with one thousand yards of black velvet. Later it was said that the expenses would not come to more than £10,000 —no doubt a Tory rumour. Some one had heard that the Earl of Godolphin was going to pay for it; and this, too, sounds like a Tory rumour, intended to glance at the notorious meanness of the Duchess. But £10,000 or £30,000, what was the difference? The Duke was obviously going to have a magnificent funeral, whoever paid for it; such a funeral as one might never see the like of again. To tell the truth, the Londoner had not had much of this sort of amusement lately. There had been the execution of the condemned lords after the Rebellion of 1715, and one or two fairly impressive burials; but the new King from Germany was not a good hand at pageantry or the art of making spectacular appearances among his people, and there was an undoubted shortage of first-class public spectacles. This one, however, promised to be really magnificent, an affair that one would probably talk about to one's grandchildren; a great occasion.

Still, it was a Whig affair, and in the midst of the public excitement a few Tories did manage to keep their heads. It is never easy when a crowd of people is pouring along the street, all bent upon reaching the same point, to keep your solitary course in the opposite direction. But some one writing on July 21 for Applebee's *Weekly Journal* managed to do just this. The evidence is not conclusive, but there is good reason for believing that this solitary critic who refused to be impressed by the approaching obsequies was Daniel Defoe; the style is certainly his, and he is known to have been writing for Applebee at this time. Whoever he was, the writer had obviously grown tired of the dreadful fuss that was being made over the dead Duke. It is true that he was addressing the readers of a Tory journal, but what he had to say far transcends the bickering of party politics; the tone of contempt for an elaborate manifestation of worldly pomp seems to arise quite genuinely out of the circumstances. "Where are the Ashes of a Caesar," he asks, and the remains of a Pompey, a Scipio, or a Hannibal?

> All are vanish'd—they and their Monuments are moulder'd into Earth—their Dust is lost, and their Place knows them no more. . . . We are now solemnizing the Obsequies of the Great Marlborough; all his Victories, all his Glories, his great projected Schemes of War, his uninterrupted Series of Conquests, which are call'd his, as if he alone had fought, and conquer'd by his Arm what so many valiant Men obtain'd for him with their Blood. All is ended where other Men, and indeed where all Men ended: HE IS DEAD!
>
> Not all his immense Wealth, the Spoils and Trophies of his Enemies, the Bounty of his grateful Mistress, and the Treasures amass'd in War and Peace; not all the mighty bulk of Gold—which some suggest is such, and so great, as I care not to mention—could either give him Life, or continue it one Moment, but HE IS DEAD; and, some say, the great Treasure he was possess'd of here had one strange particular Quality attending it—which might have been very dissatisfying to him if he had consider'd much on it—namely, that he could not carry much of it WITH HIM.
>
> We have nothing left us of this great Man that we can converse with, but his Monument, and his History. He is now number'd among things pass'd. The Funeral, as well as the Battles, of the Duke of Marlborough, are like to adorn our Houses in Sculpture as Things equally gay, and to be look'd on with pleasure. Such is the end of human Glory, and so little is the World able to do—for the greatest Men that come into it, and for the greatest Merit those Men can arrive to.
>
> What then is the Work of Life? What the Business of great Men, that pass the Stage of the World in seeming Triumph, as those Men we call Heroes have done? Is it to grow great in the mouth of Fame, and take up many Pages in History?

Alas ! that is no more than making a Tale for the reading of Posterity, till it turns into Fable and Romance. Is it to furnish Subject to the Poets, and live in their immortal Rhimes as they call them ? That is, in short, no more than to be hereafter turn'd into Ballad and Song, and be sung by old Women to quiet Children ; or, at the Corner of a Street, to gather Crowds in aid of the Pickpocket and the Whore. Or is their Business rather to add Virtue and Piety to their Glory, which alone will pass with them into Eternity, and make them truly Immortal ? . . . Let no Man envy the great and glorious Men as we call them ! Could we see them now, how many of them would move our Pity, rather than call for our Congratulations ! These few Thoughts, Sir, I send to prepare your Readers' Minds when they go to see the Magnificent Funeral of the late Duke of Marlborough.

Rather more than a week later, Atterbury, the Tory Dean of Westminster, whose office naturally compelled him to conduct the burial service in the Abbey, was writing to his friend Pope :

I go to-morrow to the Deanery, and, I believe, I shall stay there till I have said dust to dust, and shut up that last scene of pompous vanity. . . . However that be, take care that you do not fail in your appointment, that the company of the living may make me some amends for my attendance on the dead.

Happily for the public, however, there were few such kill-joys about. The great day had been fixed for August 2, but it had been postponed because four thousand medals which were being struck at the Mint would not be ready in time. Finally, however, it was arranged that the funeral should take place on August 9 ; and now, with only about a week to go, the preparations were well in hand. Scaffolding was going up in Pall Mall, and along the route by which the procession was to pass. The *Daily Journal* had been informed that the road from the Bell Tavern in King Street to the Abbey was to be boarded and lined with black cloth for the nobility and gentry to walk upon. In Hyde Park three regiments of the Foot Guards were being put through special exercises ; they were to wait for the cortege at Hyde Park Corner, and as soon as it reached that point the officers were to strike their pikes and colours, and each sentinel " to fix the muzzle of his musquet to the ground, and lean his head in a melancholly posture on the butt-end." When the corpse had passed by they were to recover sharply, reverse their arms, and march in solemn procession to the Abbey.

Meanwhile the Company of Upholders were putting up their black baize all along the route—two hundred yards of it in the Henry VII Chapel where the hero was to be buried, and lesser displays on the fronts of private houses. Tickets had been sent to all the Lords Temporal and Spiritual of Great Britain, Roman Catholics and minors excepted, inviting them to attend in person, and invitations had also been issued to a number of distinguished generals and other officers. Two days before the funeral, advertisements began to appear in the newspapers offering to let rooms which commanded a good view of the procession ; ladies and gentlemen would be carefully attended, and provided with cold dishes and the best wines, as well as tea, coffee, and chocolate. Some idea of the growing excitement may be gathered from the *Daily Journal :*

> The extraordinary Preparations that are making for Solemnizing the Funeral Obsequies of the late Duke of Marlborough, have so raised the Expectation of the Curious, that every Bulk, Walk, Window, and Foot of Earth within View of the Procession is Contracted for, and 'tis believed that even the Royal Horse at Charing Cross must be oblig'd on this Occasion to carry Double.

So far most of the Tory newspapers had maintained a glum silence about the approaching celebration, but on Saturday, August 4, *Mist's Journal* came out with a really determined attack on the dead hero. His sister's frailty with James II was once more produced to explain his rapid rise to favour; he was accused of cowardice—"His conduct was not over-heated with too much personal courage"; he was sneered at for deserting James II in his hour of defeat. And this was only the first instalment; a sequel was promised for the following week. But the sequel never appeared. In the interval Government messengers had made an unexpected visit to the printing-house, seized all the papers that they could lay their hands on, and taken the printers off to prison. A sadly attenuated *Journal* appeared the following Saturday with a facetious apology for not continuing the account of Marlborough's career:

> We must beg our Readers' Pardon for not continuing, as we design'd, the CHARACTER begun in our Last; certain Gentlemen, with GREYHOUNDS at their Breasts, having seiz'd our Materials, desiring, as 'tis supposed, to have the first reading of our Memoirs.

Still, Mist had made his protest, even though a hand was clapped over his mouth before he had finished what he had to say. But even Mist's scorn for the dead Whig hero was not so bitter as that of the *London Journal* some weeks later. Discreetly naming no names, it made a venomous attack on those mock-heroes who have a violent appetite for war and victory, but who are valorous by proxy and keep out of all danger themselves:

> This was the prudent Bravery of a late great Conqueror, who was never tir'd of War, and yet never tir'd himself in it: In the Heat of a Battle fought for his Glory, he run no Risque, but sate securely at a great Distance with the wise old Woman his Mistress, waiting for Laurels of other People's winning.

But John Churchill, so sensitive to such attacks while he was alive, had now passed beyond the malice of his enemies. His embalmed body lay in state in his darkened house at St. James's. Wax candles burnt all day and all night beside his coffin, and the great chamber where it rested was hung with black velvet and carpeted with baize. At the far end of the chamber, raised three steps above the level of the floor, stood the great bed of state; the tester was adorned with black plumes, and there was a majesty escutcheon at the head. The coffin, which was covered with crimson velvet, had a fine Holland sheet spread over it; on the sheet there lay a pall of black velvet. And on the pall the upholders had laid a complete suit of armour, with a general's truncheon clasped in the right hand, the Garter and the George hung about the neck, and a rich sword in a scabbard of crimson velvet buckled to the side. On the right hand they had set a ducal coronet; on the left, the cap of a Prince of the Empire. The helmet rested upon a cushion of crimson velvet adorned with gold fringes and tassels; the feet had been placed upon a lion couchant holding a banner with the Duke's arms. The whole house was in the deepest mourning, and two other rooms had been hung entirely in black for the reception of the nobility.

The distinguished mourners who had been invited to attend at the house on Thursday, August 9, had been asked to arrive by eleven o'clock, as the procession was timed to start at noon precisely. Actually, however, the usual delays occurred, and it was not until half-past twelve that it began to leave the house and move slowly away through St. James's Park towards Hyde Park Corner. From there the route lay along Piccadilly, and down St. James's Street into Pall Mall, and so on to Charing Cross, and along King Street to the Abbey. At Hyde Park Corner the Army was waiting to go through the exercises that it had been practising in the Park for several weeks. When the cortege appeared, the officers duly stuck their colours, and the sentinels leant their heads in a melancholy posture on the butt ends of their musquets. Then, at the word of command, the troops sprang to attention, and from that point they led the procession to the Abbey.

First came a detachment of the Horse-Grenadiers, followed by two troops of the Horse-Guards, and then two companies of cannoneers and bombardiers, with fifteen cannon and two mortars, and with the great kettle-drums of the artillery on a carriage drawn by two horses. They were followed in their turn by three detachments of the Foot-Guards, all in military mourning, with their arms reversed, their colours furled and wrapped in cypress cloth, their drums smothered with black baize and escutcheons, and their trumpets covered with cypress and adorned with Marlborough's banners. So far the procession was only repeating on a more elaborate scale the ordinary military funerals of the day. But now came a group of generals, nine of them. Some of those had fought under Marlborough, and one or two of them were themselves distinguished soldiers, notably Wade and Wills. And finally, prancing along in all the magnificence of his rank and attracting attention from every quarter, came that fine old campaigner, the Earl of Cadogan, Marlborough's friend and Quarter-Master-General for many years, and now upon his death the Commander-in-Chief of His Majesty's forces and Master of the Ordnance. It was afterwards reported by his enemies that Cadogan's bearing on this important occasion was not marked by that solemn appearance of grief which might have been expected of him, and that he seemed to be delighting more in his new honours than mourning the occasion for them. Atterbury, who disliked him, gave currency to this rumour in a ruthless epigram :

> Ungrateful to the ungrateful man he grew by,
> A bad, bold, blustering, bloody, blundering booby.

But soldiers are mercurial fellows, and it was perhaps too much to expect that Cadogan, riding along in his magnificent uniform, should look consistently depressed at every point in the long and spectacular journey to the Abbey. He was attended by his Quarter-Master-General, his Adjutant-General, and by six aides-de-camp. A company of Grenadiers from the first regiment of Guards completed the Army's contribution to the day's pageantry.

But though the Army had now done its bit, the procession was only beginning. The arrangements for the funeral had been carried out by the College of Heralds ; and now, at a proper distance from the last line of soldiers, came the Heralds' Porter in a gown of cloth with a black staff, accompanied by eight Conductors similarly clothed. These were followed in due course by seventy-three old pensioners from Chelsea, marching two and two, the first one single : seventy-three old soldiers to represent the Duke's years upon earth. Far behind them, the rest of the enormous procession wound slowly along with its banners and plumes between the rows of tall houses. Looking down from windows and balconies, the spectators could see bright spots of moving colour in this sluggish stream of mourning, the scarlet tunic of an officer, the glint of a helmet or a bridle, the blue and white of a drooping banner. From the street below came the slow tramp of men marching, the sharp clop of horses' hooves, and the steady murmur of the gazing crowd :

Two trumpeters on horseback.
A kettle-drum.
Two trumpeters on horseback.
A kettle-drum.
Major Gardiner bearing the first standard on a lance, supported by two officers.

The first Mourning Horse, led by a groom and covered in black cloth reaching to the ground.

Forty mourners in black cloaks, knights, esquires and gentlemen, riding two and two.
Rouge Croix Pursuivant at Arms.
The Guidon on a lance, borne by Major Keightley, supported by two officers.

The second Mourning Horse.

Forty mourners in black cloaks, the servants of noblemen, riding two and two, with black hat-bands and black gloves.
Two trumpeters with the banners of Woodstock.
Rouge Dragon Pursuivant at Arms.
The banner of Woodstock on a lance, borne by Lieutenant-Colonel Purcell, supported by two officers.

The third Mourning Horse.

Two trumpeters with the banners of a Prince of the Empire.
Blue Mantle Pursuivant at Arms.
The banner of the Duke as a Prince of the Empire, borne by Colonel Petyt, supported by two officers.

The fourth Mourning Horse, adorned with the Duke's arms as a Prince of the Empire.

Forty mourners on horseback in black cloaks, servants of the Duke, riding two and two.
The Duke's secretary, by himself.
The Duke's two chaplains.
Two trumpeters in His Majesty's livery with banners of the Order of the Garter.
Portcullis Pursuivant at Arms.
The banner of the Order of the Garter on a lance, borne by Colonel Pendlebury, supported by two officers.

The fifth Mourning Horse, adorned with the arms of the Garter.

Forty mourners in black cloaks, servants of the Duke, riding two and two.
The Duke's four great officers: his Chamberlain, his Steward, his Treasurer, his Comptroller.
Three trumpeters in His Majesty's livery.
The Chester Herald of Arms.
The great banner of the Duke's full arms on a lance, borne by Colonel Hopkey, supported by two officers.

The chief Mourning Horse, adorned with feathers, stars, and escutcheons, covered to the ground in mourning velvet caparisoned with the Duke's arms, and led by an equerry assisted by a groom.

The spurs and gauntlets of the Duke, borne by the Somerset Herald.
His helmet and crest, borne by the Lancaster Herald.
His target and sword, borne by the Windsor Herald.
His surcoat of arms, borne by Norroy King of Arms.

And now at last, drawn by eight horses covered with velvet, the magnificent funeral chariot. Surmounted by waving plumes and trophies of war, it had been visible to the dense crowds long before it drew near. On both sides it was adorned with shields representing the Duke's victories, and underneath was a scroll in huge letters: BELLO HAEC ET PLURA. On the right of it rode five captains in scarlet tunics, and on the left five more, bearing aloft bannerols that showed the descent and lineage of the Duke. Each of the eight horses was led by a groom in mourning dress. The coffin lay as on a great bed of state for all to see. The canopy above it was supported by four columns; it was of black velvet, lined with taffeta and adorned with a deep gold fringe and tassels at each of its four corners. Upon the coffin, as before, rested a complete suit of armour. The dead Duke still lay in state, but now all London was looking on. Two gentlemen of his bedchamber sat bare-headed beside the coffin, one at the head, the other at the foot. It was only a dead body that they were taking along the street, but there is a strange virtue in cold clay, that can stiffen every limb and dull every eye as it is carried past. One recovers soon enough, no doubt, but even on a summer day there is a cold air surrounding a hearse, and the living are less alive for having met it.

Immediately behind the funeral chariot walked Captain Reed, the Duke's Master of Horse, leading by a silken rein a horse of honour which was covered with cloth of gold and adorned with black plumes and white. And behind him Garter King of Arms, carrying in his right hand his rod of office, as director of the funeral. The pageantry was now almost concluded; but there was still a long train of mourning coaches to go by. In the first of those sat the chief mourner, the Duke of Montagu, a son-in-law of the dead Duke, with his train-bearer, Sir Robert Rich. In the second coach came the Earls of Godolphin and Sunderland; the first of those was also a son-in-law, and the young Earl of Sunderland, who had succeeded his father only a few weeks before Marlborough's death, was a grandson. But a fourth noble lord who might also have been expected to attend was noticeably absent: there was no Duke of Bridgwater. The Duke had married one of Marlborough's daughters, but she had died some years ago. No doubt he could not mourn her indefinitely, but he had chosen an odd time to take a second wife, for on the Sunday before the funeral of his father-in-law he had been married to a sister of the Duke of Bedford. No doubt the Duke, who was not an impetuous young lover, could have waited a few days longer if he had wished; one can only suppose that he did not wish.

There followed seven more coaches with fourteen noble Dukes and Earls who were taking an official part in the ceremony, and then, as a final concession to the picturesque, a second Horse of Honour, led by Captain Fish. After that there was still the King's coach, and the coach of the Prince of Wales, though neither King nor Prince was there in person, and a long succession of lesser coaches containing the nobility and gentry according to their various degrees. And finally, to close the procession, a troop of one hundred Horse-Guards.

All this time the guns at the Tower had been firing, one every minute; and this gloomy and impressive sound continued to reverberate through the streets and alleys and rattle the windows until the body was finally laid in its tomb. When at last the procession reached the Abbey, it was met by the rival pageantry of the Dean and Chapter, and the chief mourners followed the coffin into the splendour of King Henry VII's Chapel. Here the choir sang an anthem specially composed for the occasion by the celebrated Bononcini, and the Dean read the burial service. When at last, about six o'clock, the body was lowered into the grave, the Chamberlain,

Steward, Comptroller, and Treasurer of the dead man broke their staves of offices and handed the pieces to Garter King of Arms, who threw them in upon the coffin. Now at last the long ceremony was over, and three rockets were sent up from the roof of the Abbey as a signal to the troops who were waiting on parade in St. James's Park. They responded immediately with a treble discharge of artillery and small arms, performed in excellent order. Several of the officers, and even some of the private soldiers, of the first regiment of Foot-Guards, Marlborough's own regiment, were observed to shed tears as they passed under the wall of his garden on their way back to camp.

The great day had passed off with scarcely a hitch. Some scaffolding had collapsed near Whitehall, but nobody was seriously hurt. One Joseph Bailey, a hackney coachman, had cause to remember the afternoon with bitterness, for he lost his licence through whipping a guardsman in Pall Mall. He was lucky to lose no more than his licence. There were, it is true, one or two other and more significant ripples of discontent. While the funeral was in progress, a number of printed papers, wresting scriptural texts from their context in such a way as to blacken the Duke's memory, were unobtrusively dropped about the streets; and several female ballad-sellers were committed to Bridewell for singing rascally ballads about him. But what a day it had been! What a day of memories! The Earl of Cadogan, big, burly, and resplendent on his prancing horse, the seventy-three old soldiers marching sturdily along, two and two, Portcullis Pursuivant, and Blue Mantle, and Norroy King at Arms, the Horse of Honour covered with cloth of gold, the trumpeters, and the great funeral chariot with its plumes and escutcheons, its velvet and taffeta, its crimson and sable and gold! There was one little boy, not yet five years old, who stood at a window and watched it all, and who remembered it many years afterwards when he was recalling to memory the impressive sights that he had seen in his time. That little boy was Horace Walpole. But there was another boy, almost six years old, and a friend of Walpole's in later years, who may also have seen this famous procession, and who may have had it in mind when he was writing his still more famous *Elegy* :

> The boast of heraldry, the pomp of pow'r,
> And all that beauty, all that wealth e'er gave,
> Awaits alike th'inevitable hour.
> The paths of glory lead but to the grave.

If Thomas Gray was indeed taken to see the great procession go by—and his parents were Londoners, and not likely to miss it—he probably never forgot the experience. Here was all the boast of heraldry, the pomp of power, and all that wealth and a Duchess could do.

It was some time before the funeral of Marlborough ceased to be a memorable occasion in the public mind. For several weeks the cynical were diverted by a squabble between the Dean of Westminster and an undertaker over the funeral pall, valued at £100, which had covered the Duke's coffin. Atterbury, who had written so grandly to Pope about the vanity of those funereal pomps, was now claiming the pall as the property of the Abbey ; the undertaker insisted that it was his. Was this a ruse of Atterbury's to make the Duchess appear contemptible ? Apparently she had only hired the magnificent pall ; it may be that Atterbury wanted to advertise that fact. At all events he persisted in his claim, and the undertaker was compelled to file a bill in Chancery to recover it. In such ignoble squabbles the life of mortal men came trickling back to its accustomed channels. The imposing pageantry was over, the dignity and the glory had departed. Man has his moments, but they are no more than that; he can make his fine gesture, but it is not to be frozen into an attitude of eternal grace. Nobility of that sort is only for the dead.

More than thirteen years later there was a last sharp echo of this great funeral. In 1735 the Duchess of Buckingham, a natural daughter of James II, and in her way as great a lady as Sarah, Duchess of Marlborough, lost her last surviving son. He died in Rome, and she had his body brought back to England for burial in the Abbey. She was naturally a vain and ostentatious woman, and to her inherent love of display there was now added the grief of a mother burying her only child, and that child a grandson of an English king. The occasion called for magnificence. Casting about for a suitable way to honour her dead boy and at the same time to gratify her own vanity, she remembered the great triumphal chariot in which the body of Marlborough had been borne to the Abbey. She wrote to his widow, asking her if she might borrow it for her own sad occasion. The reply of the Duchess of Marlborough was brief and final: "It carried my Lord Marlborough, and shall never be profaned by any other corpse." The Duchess of Buckingham, the daughter of a king, had stooped to sue; she now remembered who she was. "I have consulted the undertaker," she wrote in her turn, "and he tells me that I may have a finer for twenty pounds."

And somewhere between the angry bickerings of those two enraged old women the mild and deprecating ghost of Marlborough was hovering in harmless protest. But life had reasserted itself; and in the trivial wind of that feminine altercation his victorious banners stirred rather sadly for the last time, and then hung motionless in the final defeat of death.

Bibliographical Notes

BURRIDGE THE BLASPHEMER

THE main source for Burridge's life up to 1712 is his own *Religio Libertini* (1712). An account of the ill-fated expedition to the West Indies in which he took part will be found in Sir Francis Wheler's *A Journal kept by Sir Francis Wheler, Knight . . .* (*Portland MSS.*, vol. iii, pp. 516–28).

The following references relate to documents in the Public Record Office bearing on his later career :—

S.P. 35/14/23 (letter) ; S.P. 35/15/20 ; S.P. 35/21/15 (warrant for his arrest) ; S.P. 35/22/37, 61, 66, 83 (letters) ; S.P. 35/23/33(3). Entry Book, 79A, Dec. 30, 1718, Jan. 14, 1719.

Various references to Burridge appear in contemporary newspapers, e.g. :—

(*Mawson's*) *Weekly Journal*, May 5, 1715 ; *Postscript to the Weekly Journal*, July 27, 1715 ; (*Read's*) *Weekly Journal*, Jan. 11, March 8, Dec. 27, 1718 ; (*Mist's*) *Weekly Journal*, March 8, 158, 171, June 11, 1720 ; *St. James's Weekly Journal, on Hanover Postman*, Dec. 19, 1719 ; *The Daily Post*, May 16, 18, 1720 ; (*Applebee's*) *Weekly Journal*, May 7, June 25, 1720 ; *Post-Boy*, June 25, 1720.

Burridge's published works include the following :—

The Consolation of Death, 1700 ; *Hell in an Uproar*, 1700 ; *The Shoemaker beyond his Last*, 1700 ; *Religio Libertini ; or, The Faith of a Converted Atheist*, 1712 ; *A New Review of London*, 1722.

JOHN LACY AND THE MODERN PROPHETS

Lacy's connection with the Prophets may be studied in the following works :—

Enthusiastick Impostors, by Richard Kingston, 1707, 1709 ; *The Honest Quaker*, 1707 (B.M. 695 *c.* 7(5)) ; *A Brand pluck'd from the Burning*, S. Keimer, 1718 ; *An Historical Account of My Own Life*, Edmund Calamy, 1821, vol. ii, pp. 71–8, 94–114.

Lacy and his fellow-prophets produced a considerable body of literature, most of which contains matter of biographical interest. See especially : *A Cry from the Desart . . . with a Preface by John Lacy, Esq.*, 1707 ; *The Prophetical Warnings of John Lacy*, 1707 ; *A Relation of the Dealings of God to*

... *John Lacy*, 1708 ; *Mr. Lacy's Letter to the Reverend Dr. Josiah Woodward*, 1708 ; *Predictions concerning the Raising of the Dead Body of Mr. Thomas Emes* (1708) ; *An Answer to Several Treatises* . . . Sir Richard Bulkeley, 1708 ; *An Impartial Account of the Prophets*, 1708 ; *The Warnings of the Eternal Spirit*, A. Whitro, 1709 ; *A Letter from J. Lacy to T. Dutton* . . . (1711).

Attacks and satirical reflections on the Prophets were numerous. See especially : *An Account of the Trial . . . of E. Marion*, 1707 ; *A Caveat against New Prophets*, Edmund Calamy, 1708 ; *The Falsehood of the New Prophets Manifested*, Henry Nicholson, 1708 ; *The New Pretenders to Prophecy*, N. Spinckes, 1708 ; *Esquire Lacy's Reasons why Dr. Emms was not Raised from the Dead*, *The Mighty Miracle* (both reprinted in *Harleian Miscellany*, vol. vi) ; *An Appeal from the Prophets to their Prophecies*, 1708 ; *The Wonderful Narrative*, 1742.

See also, *Flying Post*, May 27, 1708 ; *A Weekly Review*, April 24, June 10, 12, 1708 ; N. Luttrell's *Brief Historical Relation of State Affairs*, vol. vi, 240, 244, 307, 571.

DR. SWIFT IN LONDON

The chief source throughout is *The Journal to Stella* (*Everyman* edition), supplemented by *The Correspondence of Jonathan Swift*, ed. F. E. Ball, and *The Letters of Jonathan Swift to Charles Ford*, ed. D. Nichol Smith. Of the numerous studies of Swift I have found R. Quintana's *The Mind and Art of Jonathan Swift* most useful for my purpose.

THE LAST YEARS OF JOSEPH ADDISON

B.M. Egerton MSS. 1971-4.

D.N.B.; *The Life of Joseph Addison*, Lucy Aikin, 1843 ; *Anecdotes*, J. Spence (ed. S. W. Singer, 1820) ; *Conjectures on Original Composition*, E. Young, 1759 ; *The Correspondence of Jonathan Swift*, ed. F. E. Ball, vol. i, pp. 188-9, ii, pp. 394-5, iii, pp. 2-4, 15-16 ; *The Works of Alexander Pope*, ed. Elwin and Courthope, vol. ix, p. 388 ; H. M. C., *Portland MSS.*, vol. v, pp. 548, 549.

A number of anecdotes of doubtful validity are to be found in *A Historical Essay on Mr. Addison*, T. Tyers, 1783, and in *Addisoniana*, 2 vols., 1843.

MISS ADDISON

B.M. Egerton MSS. 1971-4.

Gentleman's Magazine, vol. lxvii, pp. 256, 385 ; *Notes and Queries*, X Series, vol. i, pp. 88, 149 ; XI Series, vol. x, p. 268 ; *Beauties of England and Wales*, 1814, vol. xv, p. 83; *Homes and Haunts of the Most Eminent British*

Poets, W. Howitt, 1857, pp. 83-93 ; *The Letters and Works of Lady Mary Wortley Montagu*, ed. Lord Wharncliffe, vol. i, pp. 59-60.

For Alexander Denton : *The Judges of England*, E. Foss, vol. viii, pp. 119-20 ; *Diary of the Earl of Egmont*, vol. iii, p. 270.

For Sir John Bridgeman : *Complete Baronetage*, ed. G. E. C., vol. iii, p. 27.

For General Cholmondeley (afterwards Earl of Cholmondeley) : *D.N.B.; Complete English Peerage*, ed. G. E. C., vol. iii, pp. 202-3.

For the Hon. John Dawnay : *Complete English Peerage*, ed. G. E. C., vol. iv, p. 452 ; *Diary of the Earl of Egmont*, vol. i, pp. 191-2 ; vol. iii, p. 160.

For Sir William Keyte : *Complete Baronetage*, vol. iii, pp. 140-1 ; *Extinct Baronetage*, p. 289 ; *London Magazine*, vol. x, p. 464.

For Sir Brian Broughton : *Complete Baronetage*, vol. iii, p. 175.

YOUNG MATTHEWS

For the actual trial of Matthews the chief source is *A Complete Collection of State Trials*, T. B. Howell, vol. xv, pp. 1323-1403.

Documents relating to his arrest and imprisonment are preserved in the Public Record Office :—

S.P. 35/12/33, 77 ; S.P. 35/14/41 ; S.P. 35/16/140 ; S.P. 35/17/117 ; S.P. 35/18/70, 72, 101, 105, 125 ; S.P. 35/19/3, 9, 10, 21, 26, 31, 50, 54 ; S.P. 35/24/73. Entry Book, 79A, Feb. 19, 1718.

The following broadsheets and pamphlets are also preserved in the Public Record Office :—

Vox Populi (S.P. 35/19/52).

A Letter from Mr. John Matthews . . . to Mr. John Broderick (S.P. 35/18/78).

The Last Dying Words . . . of Mr. John Matthews (S.P. 35/19/47).

Mr. John Matthews, the Printer, His last Farewel to the World (S.P. 35/19/51).

The following pamphlet is in the British Museum :—

The Declaration of John Matthews, Delivered to a Friend two Days before his Death (1850 *c.* 10(52)).

References to Matthews occur in the following newspapers : (*Read's*) *Weekly Journal*, May 10, 1718, Oct. 31, Nov. 7, 21, 1719 ; (*Mist's*) *Weekly Journal*, July 19, 1718, Sept. 26, Oct. 31, Nov. 21, 1719 ; (*Applebee's*) *Weekly Journal*, July 19, 1718, July 18, 25, Aug. 9, 16, Sept. 26, Nov. 14, 1719 ; June 25, 1720 ; *The Orphan Reviv'd*, Sept. 12, Oct. 24, Nov. 14, 1719 ; *Weekly Medley*, Sept. 19, Nov. 7, 14, 1719, Jan. 16, 1720 ; *Daily Post*, Nov. 4, 10, 11, 13, 1719 ; *Whitehall Evening Post*, Nov. 7, 1719 ; *Flying Post*, Nov. 12, 1719 ; *St. James's Weekly Post*, Nov. 14, 1719 ; *Ludlow Postman*, Feb. 19, 1720 ; *Post-Boy*, June 25, 1720.

THE FUNERAL OF JOHN, DUKE OF MARLBOROUGH

The information on which this account is based has been drawn almost entirely from contemporary London newspapers published between the date of Marlborough's death (June 16, 1722) and his funeral on August 9. The official account of the funeral procession given in *The London Gazette*, Aug. 7-11, 1722, differs in some points of detail from that given in *The Order of the Procession at the Funeral of . . . John, Duke of Marlborough.* This pamphlet, a copy of which may be found in the British Museum (G, 14129(6)) was probably intended to serve as an official programme for the ceremony.

See also *The Works of Alexander Pope,* ed. Elwin and Courthope, vol. ix, pp. 50, 52 ; *Letters of Horace Walpole,* ed. Mrs. Paget Toynbee, vol. x, p. 453.

PRINTED IN GREAT BRITAIN AT THE UNIVERSITY PRESS, ABERDEEN